THE FIRST WORLD WAR 1914–18

BOOK ONE

WAR BEYOND BRITAIN

8

THE FIRST WORLD WAR 1914–18

BOOK ONE

WAR BEYOND BRITAIN

FIONA REYNOLDSON

Heinemann Educational Books

Acknowledgements

COVER: 'The Menin Road' by Paul Nash.
TITLE PAGE PHOTOGRAPH: *Indian soldiers at Alexandria in 1915. They are about to load their mules and food. They are going to Gallipoli.*

Other uniform titles:

Twentieth-Century British History
  Book 1   1900–14
  Book 2   1919–39
  Book 3   1945 to the 1980s
  all by Fiona Reynoldson
War at Home by Fiona Reynoldson
War in Europe by Fiona Reynoldson
War in the Far East by Fiona Reynoldson
The USA in the Twentieth Century by
  Andrew Reid
Britain's Industrial Revolution by
  Jacqueline Roberts
Ships by Clive Booth

Heinemann Educational Books Ltd
22 Bedford Square, London WC1B 3HH

LONDON EDINBURGH MELBOURNE
AUCKLAND SINGAPORE KUALA LUMPUR
NEW DELHI IBADAN NAIROBI
JOHANNESBURG PORTSMOUTH [NH]
KINGSTON

© Fiona Reynoldson 1987

First published 1987

British Library Cataloguing in Publication Data

Reynoldson, Fiona
   The First World War 1914–18.
   Book 1: War beyond Britain
   1. World War, 1914–1918
   I. Title
   940.3   D522.7

   ISBN 0–435–31744–X

Filmset and printed in Great Britain by
BAS Printers Limited, Over Wallop,
Hampshire

The author and publishers would like to thank the following for permission to reproduce illustrations on the pages indicated:

BBC Hulton Picture Library: pp. 11, 27, 38, 56, 65, 66 (top), 69 (top) and 85 (lower).
The British Library, Newspaper Library: p. 89.
Imperial War Museum: cover; title page; pp. 3, 8, 9, 15, 17, 18, 22, 31, 32, 33, 39, 42, 52, 54, 57, 58, 59, 60, 61, 62, 72, 73 (lower), 78, 82 and 87 (top).
The Mansell Collection: pp. 5, 6, 66 (lower), and 83.
Mary Evans Picture Library: pp. 21, 30, 64, 69 (lower) and 85 (top).
Peter Newark's Historical Pictures: pp. 23, 45 and 46–7.
Popperfoto: pp. 16, 24, 36, 51 and 81.
Punch Publications: p. 1.
Syndication International: p. 55.
The Tank Museum, Bovington: p. 75.
Topham: p. 73 (top).

Artwork by Ian Foulis

Contents

1 The Great Countries of Europe

There were many great countries in Europe. They did not always get on well together.

Reasons for war in 1914

5

1 For a long time Britain had been the richest country in the world. It owned land all over the world. By 1900 Germany was rich and strong. Germany wanted to own more land. Britain and Germany were rivals.

10

2 Germany had taken land from France. That was in 1871. France wanted the land back. France was afraid that Germany might take more of its land.

3 Germany was in the middle of Europe

15

(see map on page 2). France, Britain and Russia could all attack it. Germany was surrounded.

4 Austria had a large empire in Europe. It was called Austria–Hungary. Many

20

different people lived in the Austrian empire. There were Slavs, for example. Many of these people wanted to be free. They did not want to be ruled by Austria. Austria was afraid that the

25

Slavs would break up its empire.

5 Germany decided to build many ships. After all it was a great country now. Germany felt it should own land all over the world. It had been pushed

30

about by Britain and France for too long.

6 Britain had thousands of ships. It needed the ships to trade all over the world. Britain did not want to share its

35

land or trade with Germany. Britain decided to build more and more ships.

Mr Punch is the photographer. He is speaking to the German sailor (who is drawn to look like the German kaiser). Mr Punch says, 'Just a little further back, please, Sir. Your shadow still interferes with the group.' Look carefully at the cartoon. Then answer the following questions:

1 *The sailors represent France, Britain and Germany. Which is which?*
2 *How do you know the French and British are friends? Find two things that tell you.*
3 *'Germany feels left out.' Is this true or false?*

The cartoon is from a magazine called Punch. *Look at the way the artist has drawn the sailors. Which sailor looks the biggest, the toughest, the most confident? Do you think the artist was French, British or German?*

Map labels:
NORWAY
SWEDEN
DENMARK
NETHERLANDS
RUSSIA
BRITAIN
GERMANY
BELGIUM
LUXEMBURG
FRANCE
AUSTRIA-HUNGARY
THE BALKANS
ITALY
PORTUGAL
SPAIN
SWITZERLAND
TURKEY

Triple Alliance: Germany, Austria–Hungary, Italy

Triple Éntente: France, Britain, Russia

Neutral: Spain, Portugal, Norway, Sweden, Denmark, Belgium, the Netherlands, Switzerland, Turkey

Europe in 1914. Later Italy changed sides.

1914

In the end the great countries of Europe were all afraid of each other. Between 1900 and 1914 they argued over land. Often they came close to war. Each of the great countries looked around for friends. Look at the map. You will see how they joined together as friends. They formed two gangs. The gangs were called alliances.

Mobilization

45 The great countries had found friends.
They decided that if there was a war it
was best to attack first. So each country
made plans for mobilization.
Mobilization means getting soldiers and
50 guns to the battlefield to fight.

Timetables

Millions of people lived in Europe. Any
war would be big. Soldiers and guns would
be put on trains. This meant that
thousands of trains would be needed. The
55 trains would carry millions of soldiers.
For example, Russia called up 3 million
soldiers in August 1914.
    The generals were in charge of
mobilization. They planned the call-up of
60 soldiers and railway timetables. There
was one great disadvantage. Once the
trains started rolling towards the
battlefields they could not be stopped.
There were thousands of trains. There
65 were millions of soldiers, guns and
bandages. There were tonnes of food.
There were millions of horses. There were
thousands of lorries. Nothing could stop
them.
70   Once the army was mobilized, there
would be war. There could be no going
back.

HMS Dreadnought *in dry dock. The
battleship carried 860 sailors and could travel
at 22 knots. The armour plating was about
28 cm thick on the sides and 35 cm thick on the
decks. The* Dreadnought *carried thirty-seven
guns and five torpedo tubes. The British were
very proud of the* Dreadnought *and wanted
more big ships like it. The government thought
Britain might need fewer ships if it built more
ships like the* Dreadnought. *A popular song
was made up: 'We want eight, and we won't
wait.' Notice the very large guns and the
washing hung out to dry.*

Things to Do

1 Fill in the gaps. (*Numbers in brackets
refer to text line numbers.*)
Britain and ——————— (9) were rivals.
They both had many ships. Germany had
taken land from —————— (10).
    Austria had a large —————— (18) in
Europe. Many different —————— (20)
lived in the Austrian empire. Many of
these people wanted to be ———— (22).
    In the end the great countries of
—————— (37) were all afraid of each other.

2 Write out the sentences below. Choose the
correct word or phrase from the brackets.

Mobilization means (hanging up mobiles/
going to a disco/getting soldiers and
guns to the battlefields). The (generals/
gerbils) were in charge of mobilization.
Once the trains started rolling towards the
(battlefields/buffers) they could not be
(started/stopped/seated).

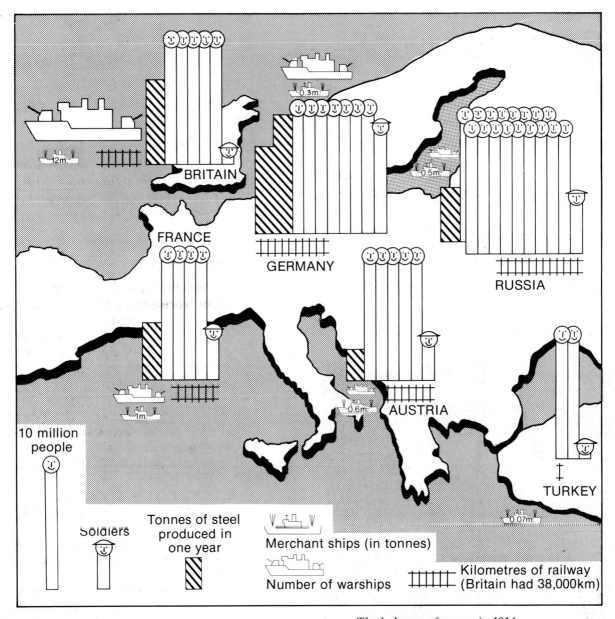

BRITAIN

FRANCE

GERMANY

RUSSIA

AUSTRIA

TURKEY

12m.

0.3m.

0.5m.

1m.

0.6m.

0.07m.

10 million people

Soldiers

Tonnes of steel produced in one year

Merchant ships (in tonnes)

Number of warships

Kilometres of railway (Britain had 38,000km)

The balance of power in 1914.

3   Trace the map of Europe on page 2. Choose two colours. Colour in the two alliances:

Britain ⎫
France ⎬ *against* ⎰ Germany
Russia ⎭   ⎱ Austria (short for Austria–Hungary)
                    Turkey (joined Germany's side)

1   *Which country had the largest population in 1914?*
2   *Which country had the largest army?*
3   *Which country had the largest navy?*
4   *Make a list of all the ways in which steel could be used in the war, e.g. to make bayonets.*
5   *Why would railways be useful in wartime?*
6   *Why did Britain need so many merchant ships?*
7   *Look carefully at the map. Try to explain in class what the balance of power meant.*

2 Sarajevo

It was 28 June 1914. The Archduke Franz
Ferdinand went to visit Sarajevo.
Sarajevo was in Bosnia. Austria owned
Bosnia. Bosnians were Slavs. Many
5   people in Bosnia hated Austria. They
wanted Bosnia to be free. A group of them
formed a secret society. They called
themselves Young Bosnia.

     The Archduke Franz Ferdinand was to
10   be the next Austrian Emperor. The Young
Bosnians wanted to kill him.

Archduke Franz Ferdinand and his wife in
Sarajevo.

The police

The police in Sarajevo were very worried.
They were afraid someone might kill the
Archduke. The army paid no attention. A
15   few policemen lined the streets.

28 June 1914

The day was warm and sunny. The
Archduke wore a bright blue tunic. It was
trimmed with gold and red.

    Six big cars drove through the streets.
20   The Archduke was in one of them. His
wife, was with him. The other
cars were full of important Austrian
people. Everyone stopped to look. One
young man was a member of the Young
25   Bosnians. His name was Cabrinovic. He
tapped a policeman on the arm.

    'Excuse me,' he said. 'Which car is the
Archduke in?'

    'That one. That one,' shouted the
30   excited policeman. He pointed to the
Archduke's car.

    Cabrinovic thanked him and turned
away. He pulled out a small bomb. He
threw it at the Archduke's car.

35   Everyone was shouting and running.
Twenty people were hurt. But the
Archduke was all right. He decided to go
on.

Change of plan

Later the Archduke wanted to visit one of
40   the wounded men. Nobody told the driver.
The driver turned the wrong way. He was
shouted at. He jammed on the brakes. He
started to go back. The car was in front of
a crowded shop. It was called Schiller's
45   Store.

Gavrilo Princip stepped forward. He took out his revolver. He fired at point blank range.

The first bullet went through the side of
50   the car. It hit the Duchess. She died immediately. The second bullet hit the Archduke in the neck. It cut the jugular vein. The Archduke died within minutes. The green feathers from his plumed hat
55   were trampled on the floor of the car.

Austria

By 11.30 a.m. on the 28 June 1914, the next Austrian Emperor and his wife lay dead. Austria was furious. It blamed Serbia. Serbia was Bosnia's neighbour. Austria
60   said that Serbian Slavs had helped the Young Bosnians and given them guns. Austria decided to crush Serbia once and for all.

The march to war

<table>
<tr><td>65</td><td>28 July</td><td>Austria declared war on Serbia. (Serbia was friends with Russia.)</td></tr>
<tr><td>70</td><td>30 July</td><td>Russia declared war on Austria. (Germany was very worried. Russia mobilized its army. Germany was sure it too would be attacked by Russia.)</td></tr>
<tr><td>75</td><td>1 August</td><td>Germany declared war on Russia. (Germany was sure France would help Russia. Germany decided to strike first.)</td></tr>
<tr><td>80
85</td><td>3 August</td><td>Germany declared war on France. (Germany wanted to defeat France quickly. German soldiers marched through Belgium. This annoyed Britain. Britain had signed a treaty. It said that Britain would fight if Belgium was attacked.)</td></tr>
<tr><td></td><td>4 August</td><td>Britain declared war on Germany.</td></tr>
</table>

Gavrilo Princip being arrested in Sarajevo in 1914. The soldiers are from the Archduke's bodyguard. The detective Spahovic is behind Princip. The student Pusic is in the peaked hat and is holding Princip's arm.

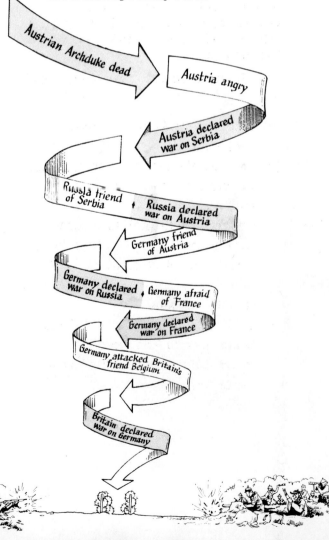

Austrian Archduke dead

Austria angry

Austria declared war on Serbia

Russia friend of Serbia — Russia declared war on Austria

Germany friend of Austria

Germany declared war on Russia — Germany afraid of France

Germany declared war on France

Germany attacked Britain's friend Belgium

Britain declared war on Germany

Things to Do

1 Fill in the gaps. (*Numbers in brackets refer to text line numbers.*)
It was the 28 June ———— (1). The Archduke Franz Ferdinand went to visit ———————— (2). Sarajevo was in —————— (3). ———————— (3) owned Bosnia. Many Bosnians wanted Bosnia to be ———— (6).

2 Gavrilo Princip was put on trial. He was questioned. This is one of the many things he was asked:

Question: Why did you shoot Archduke Franz Ferdinand?
Answer: Because people suffer so much. It is the Archduke's fault. I am a villager's son and I know how it is in the villages so I wanted to take revenge and I am not sorry.

From the translation of the text of the Sarajevo trial.

(a) Who shot the Archduke Franz Ferdinand?

(b) Write out the sentences below. Choose the correct word from the brackets.
Princip shot the Archduke because (he was mad / people suffer). Princip was the son of a (vicar / villager). Princip was (sorry / not sorry) he had shot the Archduke.

(c) Look at the photograph of Princip being arrested. Then read the following three accounts of what happened:

'I did not know whether I had shot him. I didn't even know how many shots I had fired. I wanted to kill myself and I raised my arm but the policeman grabbed me and beat me. Then bloody as I was they took me to the police station. They beat me again. They wanted revenge.'

Gavrilo Princip. From J. Remak, 'Sarajevo' (Weidenfeld & Nicolson, 1957).

'I fought my way through the crowd. Five or six men were wrestling with Princip. Two of the men were members of the Archduke's bodyguard; the others were passersby. Princip hit me a terrific blow. He didn't realize that by grabbing him I was saving him from a lynching.'

Detective Spahovic. From the translation of the text of the Sarajevo trial.

'At last Spahovic grabbed Princip and with another policeman dragged him away. Princip was vomiting because he had taken poison and had cuts from his fight with the crowd.'

A student eyewitness. From J. Remak, 'Sarajevo' (Weidenfeld & Nicolson, 1957).

Discuss in class the differences between the three accounts of what happened. Say why you think they are different.

3 How an Army Works

Armies are made up of many thousands of soldiers. The soldiers are organized into groups. The diagram shows how the British army was organized in 1914.

5   All these soldiers need food. They need clothes and boots. They need guns. They need bullets. They need rest. They need to go home on leave. They need to wash and shave. They need to go to the lavatory.

10   They need doctors, bandages and medicine.

The army had to organize everything for the soldiers – from drinking water to bombs.

15   Each soldier had a ration of food. This included meat, bacon, bread, butter, jam, tea, sugar, condensed milk, cheese, oatmeal, potatoes, vegetables (fresh or dried), tobacco or cigarettes, matches,

20   salt, pepper and mustard. All this cost 1s. 10d. (9p) for each soldier for one day.

The rations did not always reach the front line trenches.

Lord Kitchener was a famous soldier. He was made War Minister in August 1914. He organized the recruiting of thousands of soldiers.

BRITONS

"WANTS YOU"

JOIN YOUR COUNTRY'S ARMY!

GOD SAVE THE KING

Australian soldiers training in France. What weapons are they practising with?

The British army in 1914. This was the plan or model. Numbers varied. There were about 250 soldiers in a company. There were about 1,000 soldiers in a battalion. However, battalions were often under strength. They had about 800 soldiers in them. ▶

Many men joined the army in 1914. Often friends stayed together. There were whole battalions of footballers, artists, and so on, who had joined up together. Many of these battalions were almost wiped out on 1 July 1916 at the battle of the Somme.

British soldiers and lorries on the Fricourt Road, France, in 1918. The soldiers marched for 50 minutes and rested for 10 minutes every hour. They carried:

5.4 kg clothing
7.6 kg rifle and ammunition
1.2 kg trench tools
3.7 kg webbing
4.4 kg pack
2.5 kg rations/water

How much weight did a soldier carry altogether?

Things to Do

1 Fill in the gaps. (*Numbers in brackets refer to text line numbers.*)
Armies are made up of many thousands of ———————— (2). The soldiers are ————————— (2) into groups. All these soldiers need ———— (5). They need clothes and ————— (6). They need ———— (6). The army had to organize everything for the soldiers – from drinking ————— (13) to ————— (14).

2 Look at the diagram of the British army in 1914. How many soldiers were in a division? If every soldier had a letter from home every week, how many letters did a division have in a week? How many did a battalion have? How many letters did a file have?

3 If one soldier used three razor blades every month, how many razor blades did a division use in a month?

4 1s. 10d. equals about 9p. How much did it cost to feed a division for a day?

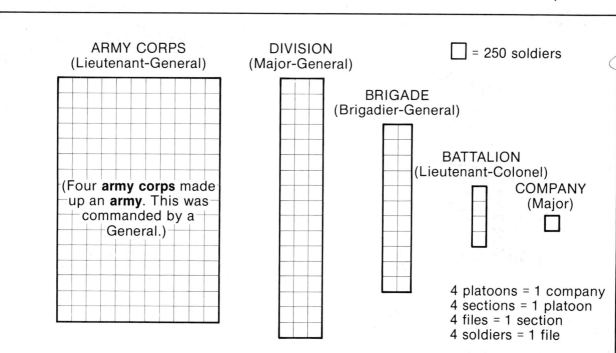

ARMY CORPS
(Lieutenant-General)

DIVISION
(Major-General)

☐ = 250 soldiers

BRIGADE
(Brigadier-General)

BATTALION
(Lieutenant-Colonel)

COMPANY
(Major)

(Four **army corps** made up an **army**. This was commanded by a General.)

4 platoons = 1 company
4 sections = 1 platoon
4 files = 1 section
4 soldiers = 1 file

4 The War of Movement, 1914

The Schlieffen Plan was the German plan to defeat France. The Germans planned to knock France out of the war. Then they could send many more soldiers to fight against Russia. They thought it would take Russia six weeks to mobilize. But the Schlieffen Plan went wrong. For one thing Russia mobilized in two weeks. However, Germany kept going.

The Schlieffen Plan.

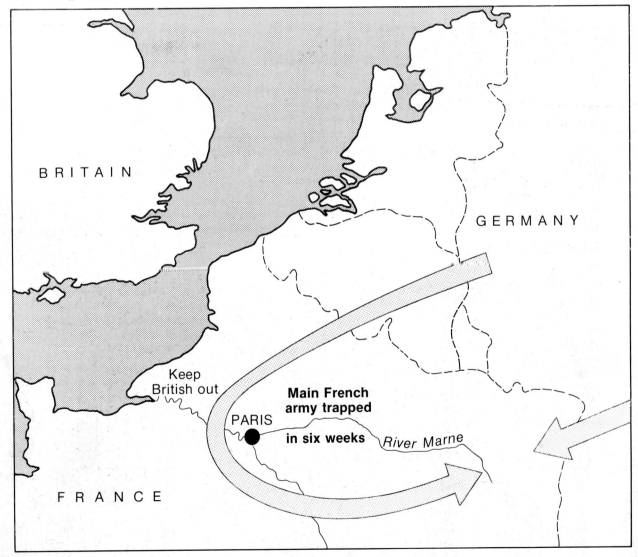

Belgium

10 The Germans needed to move quickly. They reckoned they had only six weeks, so they marched through Belgium. People in Britain and in other countries were shocked. Germany had no right to

15 march into Belgium. But Germany did.

Britain goes to war, 4 August 1914

Britain said it would help Belgium. So Britain declared war on Germany. It was eleven o'clock at night. Crowds of excited people came out on to the streets. They

20 cheered. They shouted. They celebrated. They would save Belgium. They would fight the wicked Germans. They would save Britain.

Thousands of young men rushed to join

25 the army. They rushed from boring jobs, hard lives or rich homes. They rushed to glory and excitement, and a short war.

In Germany the young men rushed to fight, too. They didn't want to miss the

30 war. The kaiser (the German king) said that his soldiers 'would be home before the leaves fall'. No one wanted to miss out. They wanted to save their country.

Recruits in December 1915.

General Joffre

General Joffre was the leader of the
35   French army. The French army rushed to
meet the Germans. Both sides fought
hard.

The British Expeditionary Force

The British Expeditionary Force (BEF)
was Britain's small, but well-trained
40   army. It was led by John French. He was
old. He was ill.

The BEF crosses to France, 9–17 August 1914

It was 9 August 1914. The BEF was made
up of 90,000 soldiers, 15,000 horses and 315
guns. They were loaded aboard ships for
45   France.

The battle of Mons (see map on page 13)

The BEF were in battle. They fought
bravely. They fought next to the French
armies. They fought to hold the Germans
back. They didn't. The German army got

What happened in 1914.

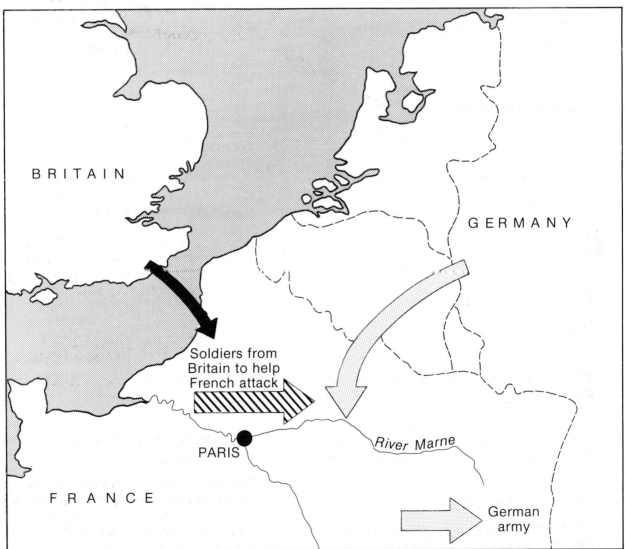

BRITAIN

GERMANY

Soldiers from
Britain to help
French attack

River Marne

PARIS

FRANCE

German
army

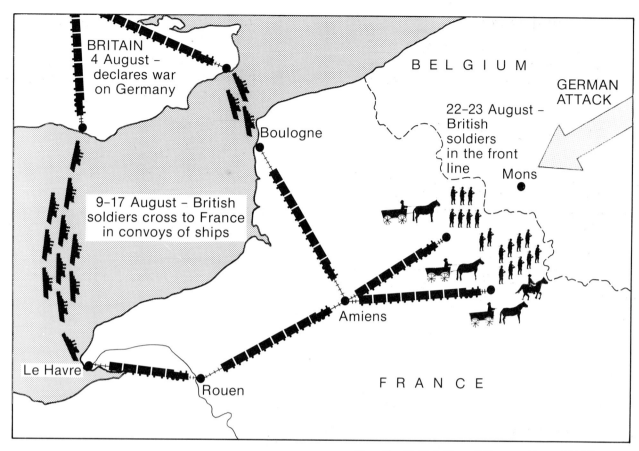

How the British Expeditionary Force (BEF) reached the front line in 1914.

50 nearer to Paris. But it was already failing. Many German soldiers were sent to fight in Russia. The German general Moltke changed the Schlieffen Plan. He tried to cut off the French armies from
55 Paris. The French were desperate. They would never give up Paris. They rushed extra soldiers from Paris. The soldiers came in taxis.

The battle of the Marne, 5–10 September

The French and British fought hard. They
60 pushed the German army back across the river Marne. (Look at the map opposite.)

The race for the sea

The Germans were stopped head on. Both sides raced northwards. The Germans
65 were trying to get round the British and French armies. The British and French were trying to stop them. Before long both sides reached the sea.

The first battle of Ypres, 12 October–11 November

There was a fierce battle at the town of Ypres.

The cost of the war of movement

70 The British lost 50,000 soldiers. The Germans lost over 100,000 soldiers. The French lost many more. And the war now seemed to have reached a stalemate. No one was winning.

Things to Do

1 Fill in the gaps. (*Numbers in brackets refer to text line numbers.*)
The Schlieffen Plan was the –––––– (1) plan to defeat –––––– (2). The Germans planned to knock –––––– (3) out of the war. Then they could send many more –––––––– (4) to fight against Russia.

2 Write down at least three reasons why young men rushed to join the army (lines 24–7).

3 Do the crossword. (*Numbers in brackets after clues refer to text line numbers. You will need to read the whole sentence to find the answer.*)

ACROSS
1 But the ––––––––– Plan went wrong. (7)
5 The French –––– rushed to meet the Germans. (35)
6 They would never give up –––––. (55)
9 He tried to ––– off the French armies from Paris. (53)
10 They pushed the German army back across the river –––––. (59)
13 They wanted –– save their country. (33)
14 The BEF ––– Britain's small, but well-trained army. (38)
15 There was a fierce battle at the town of –––––. (68)
16 The BEF was made –– of 90,000 soldiers. (42)

DOWN
1 And the war now seemed to have reached a –––––––––. (72)
2 The kaiser said that his soldiers 'would be –––– before the leaves fall'. (30)
3 The BEF were –– battle. (46)
4 The Germans planned to knock –––––– out of the war. (2)
7 –– Britain declared war on Germany. (16)
8 Many German soldiers were sent to fight –– Russia. (51)
11 They rushed ––––– soldiers from Paris. (56)
12 They didn't want to –––– the war. (29)

5 Life in the Trenches

The front line was made up of three lines, one behind the other. First was the fire trench. Second was the travel trench. Third was the support trench. All three
5 were fairly close together. Soldiers from the support trench could quickly get to the fire trench if there was a German raid. All these trenches were dug in zigzags.

Support trenches

Support trenches were more comfortable
10 than the other two trenches. They had kitchens, lavatories and stores. They had dugouts, too.

Dugouts

Five-metre shafts were dug. These led to dugout caves (2 metres high and about 4
15 metres wide). Mostly these dugouts were for officers. They were very snug. But a soldier could easily be buried alive if a shell exploded on top of the dugout.

Serving in the trenches

A division in the army was made up of
20 about 13,000–18,000 soldiers. Of these about 2,000 soldiers served in the front line at any one time. Sometimes soldiers stayed at the front line for a long time. The Black Watch was a Scottish
25 regiment of soldiers. They once served for forty-eight days without break. This was unusual.

A soldier's month

In one month a soldier would spend:

- 4 days in the front line
30 - 4 days in the support line
- 8 days in reserve
- 14 days resting

The inside of a dugout occupied by officers of a Howitzer battery in August 1917. Can you find the tin helmet, gas mask and candles?

Rest

Good sleep, baths and warm food. That was what rest meant to all soldiers. They
35 bought cigarettes. They bought egg and chips. They shared a bottle of cheap wine. They cursed the digging, repairing and drilling. Sports, concerts, and football were all part of rest. The soldiers loved
40 these.

Back in the trenches the old routine started again.

Nights

45
❝I shall not forget the nights. The blackness was broken by gun flashes, the gleam of star shells, the scream of a shell, the rattle of a machine gun. In the eery light tree stumps seemed to move, coils of wire became people. Very few of us were easy on sentry duty.❞

From F. Noakes,
'The Distant Drum' (Tunbridge Wells, 1952).

50

55
The nights were long. In winter it was very cold. Long johns, thick socks, wool vests, sheepskin jerkins, home-knitted cardigans, layers of newspapers and oiled waistcoats did not keep out the cold. The soldiers froze on duty. They froze in their shelters in the trenches. They slept badly. They waited for the sergeant to bang on the soles of their boots. It was their turn for sentry duty.

A sandbag full of rations. If the carrier fell in a shellhole, the food was mixed up, wet and filthy. Machonochie stew was meat and vegetable stew in tins. It was very tasty. Butter was in tins. Porridge and stew often arrived in screw-top jars.

Soldiers eating a meal together in a shellhole.

Morning

60
❝If you have spent the night in a muddy trench, in wet clothes with no fire, then the first gleam of sunshine at dawn is pure heaven.❞

H. Drinkwater. From Denis Winter,
'Death's Men: Soldiers of the Great War'
(Allen Lane, 1978).

And with morning came a tot of rum and breakfast.

Food

65

70
Food was a great comfort. Soldiers carried rations up to the front line. They moved in the evenings. The rations were put in sandbags. Sometimes the food did not arrive. Fighting, shelling, mud or falling into shellholes delayed or killed the soldiers bringing the food. When it did come soldiers sat down together to eat it.

Comrades

75
Out of every ten men in a trench, most soldiers said, you found one real, close friend, eight comrades and one difficult man. All these men fought together. They shared trench digging. They shared

Soldiers in a reserve trench. Notice the parapet (the higher side of the trench). How is it held up? Notice the sandbags and the lack of shelter from the weather. What are the soldiers doing? Has this area been fought over?

terror. Often they felt closer to each other than to their families.

80 ʻWe sometimes used to lie out under the stars when it was quiet. All the men in my company were from Oldham in Lancashire. They had been cotton spinners and factory workers. They talked of their homes and families and of
85 Blackpool in wakes week. What a fabulous picture of fun they painted.ʼ

From Lieutenant Henry Lawson , 'Vignettes of the Western Front' (Positif Press, 1979).

The soldiers needed the memories and the friends. There were many hardships.

The weather

The weather was everyone's enemy. The
90 British and German soldiers were not far apart. They could hear each other across no man's land. Private Stokes remembered hearing German soldiers sneezing. He heard them stamp their feet
95 to keep warm.

The mud

The mud was the worst. Nothing kept it out.

100 ʻPuttees do not stop liquid mud getting into your boots if you sink in ten inches [25 cm] or more.ʼ

Corporal L. Smith. From Denis Winter, 'Death's Men: Soldiers of the Great War' (Allen Lane, 1978).

Lice, rats and flies

ʻI sat on the latrine box and patiently counted 103 lice on my clothes and body. God how I hate the little lobsters!ʼ

A. Abraham. From Denis Winter, 'Death's Men: Soldiers of the Great War' (Allen Lane, 1978).

British soldiers billeted in a French barn. Wire netting and timber frames were put up in the barns. This meant a lot of soldiers could be fitted in, but sometimes these frames collapsed and soldiers were injured or killed.

The French villagers and British soldiers sometimes got on well and sometimes they didn't: '. . . if 3 million French soldiers came and squatted in a part of England with their lice, guns, bad language, scrounging wood for fires, blasting through hedges and banging rickety gates, then the English might not like it . . .' – R. Mottram, 'Personal Records of the War' (Scholartis, 1929).

The lice made the soldiers scratch. This
105 led to boils and ulcers. It was very
difficult to get rid of the lice. Some men
cracked the lice with thumbnails. Then
they ran a lighted candle up the seams of
their clothes (quickly!). The whole chase
110 took about two hours. Groups of friends
gathered to talk while they deloused
their clothes. They called the lice by
many names including 'chats'. This is
where the word chatting, meaning a
115 friendly talk comes from.

Rats gathered in the trenches to feed on
the food and on the dead. They were hated
and feared.

Flies were a terrible problem. An
120 infantry division had about five thousand
to six thousand horses. These horses
made forty tonnes of droppings every day.
This was a good breeding ground for flies.
Old soldiers said that the buzzing of the
125 flies drowned the noise of a shell whizzing
on a battlefield on a hot day. One soldier
counted thirty-two flies in his shaving
water. The flies rose in black clouds from
the dead bodies on the battlefield.

*After breakfast there were jobs to do. One third
of the men would be on sentry duty. One third
went to get rations. One third rested, but
resting included 'digging, filling sandbags,
carrying ammunition, scheming against water,
strengthening wire and resetting duckboards'
– F. Noakes, 'The Distant Drum' (1952). What
job do you think these soldiers are going to do?*

*If a soldier were lucky he might spend much of
the war on a quiet front.*

Death

130 Shells, gas, snipers, machine guns – all
meant death. Danger, the death of friends
and the waiting broke many soldiers.
Eyelids twitched, hands shook. Soldiers
shivered when guns fired. Some soldiers
135 broke down completely. Fear of death
and the sight of death was one of the
worst things soldiers had to live with.

    ❛The dead man lay on the earth. Never before
had I seen a man who had just been killed. His
face and body were terribly gashed and the
140 smell of blood, mixed with the fumes of the
shell, made me sick. Only a great effort
stopped my legs giving way. I saw the sick
grey faces of the file. I knew they felt the same
145 and a voice seemed to whisper in my ear,
"Why shouldn't you be next?"❜

*From 'Death's Men: Soldiers of the Great War'
(Allen Lane, 1978).*

Things to Do

1   Fill in the gaps. (*Numbers in brackets
refer to text line numbers.*)
The ----- (1) line was made up of
----- (1) lines. First was the ---- (2)
trench. Second was the ------ (3)
trench. Third was the ------- (4)
trench. Soldiers from the support trench
could ------- (6) get to the fire trench
if there was a ------ (7) raid.

2 Do the crossword. (*Numbers in brackets after some clues refer to the text line numbers. You will need to read the whole sentence to find the answer.*)

ACROSS

1 Fighting, shelling, ––– or falling into shellholes delayed or killed the soldiers bringing the food. (69)

5 –– sometimes used to lie out under the stars when it was quiet. (80)

7 The ––– made the soldiers scratch. (104)

9 ––– gathered in the trenches to feed on the food and on the dead. (116)

10 They bought ––– and chips. (35)

11 'If you have spent the night in a muddy trench, in ––– clothes with no fire, then the first gleam of sunshine at dawn is pure heaven.' (59)

13 Short for non-commissioned officer.

17 These led to ––––– caves. (13)

19 I ––– the sick grey faces of the file. (143)

20 'We sometimes used to ––– out under the stars when it was quiet.' (80)

21 Sometimes the food ––– not arrive. (68)

22 'Why shouldn't you be –––?' (146)

24 'If you have spent the night in a muddy trench, in wet clothes with – – fire, then the first gleam of sunshine at dawn is pure heaven.' (59)

25 'They talked –– their homes and families and of Blackpool in wakes week.' (84)

DOWN

1 Some ––– cracked the lice with thumbnails. (106)

2 They shared trench –––––––. (76)

3 ––– soldiers said that the buzzing of the flies drowned the noise of a shell whizzing on a battlefield on a hot day. (124)

4 'The blackness was broken by gun flashes, the gleam of star shells, the –––––– of a shell, the rattle of a machine gun.' (43)

6 'Very few of us were ––––– on sentry duty.' (48)

8 When it did come soldiers sat down together to ––– it. (71)

12 'His face and ––––– were terribly gashed and the smell of blood, mixed with the fumes of the shell, made me sick.' (139)

14 In winter it was very –––––. (49)

15 French for 'yes'.

16 Support trenches were more comfortable than the other ––– trenches. (9)

18 Out of every ––– men in a trench, most soldiers said, you found one real, close friend, eight comrades and one difficult man. (73)

19 An infantry division had about five thousand to ––– thousand horses. (119)

21 'Puttees –– not stop liquid mud getting into your boots if you sink in ten inches [25 cm] or more.' (98)

23 This led –– boils and ulcers. (104)

6 The Western Front, 1915

It was 1915. The war on the Western Front was a stalemate. Nothing moved. The French and British soldiers sat in their trenches. The German soldiers sat in their trenches. They stared at each other across no man's land.

— The Western Front

The trenches stretched from the English Channel to Switzerland. The distance was several hundred kilometres.

'Stand to'

There were two dangerous times of day – the first light of dawn and the twilight of dusk. Enemy soldiers could attack. They could not be seen easily.

❝ About half an hour or so before dawn and dusk the order "stand to" was given and silently passed along the whole front. Suddenly, a German machine gun lets rip. A Vickers gun returns the fire from our side. Then there's rifle fire, just to let Jerry know we're awake and it's no bloody use starting anything. Jerry does the same, for it is the morning hate. ❞

From George Coppard, 'With a Machine Gun to Cambrai' (HMSO, 1969).

Breakfast

Breakfast came after the morning 'stand to'. Often it was bacon sizzling in the frying pan and hot tea. Then the soldiers did their jobs for the day. They cleaned their rifles. They dug new trenches. They mended old trenches. All the time they kept their heads down. They were soon killed by enemy snipers if they didn't.

❝ Lulled by the quietness, someone is foolish and lingers with his head above the parapet. Then, like a puppet whose strings have suddenly snapped, he crashes to the bottom of the trench. A pal of mine, Bill Bailey, died this way when we were cooking up breakfast. ❞

From George Coppard, 'With a Machine Gun to Cambrai' (HMSO, 1969).

There were millions of soldiers in the trenches. They could not go on living this way for ever. After all, this was war. Someone had to win. Someone had to move. Someone had to drive the other side away.

The Germans had already moved into France. They just needed to stay put. The French and British needed to drive the Germans out. They needed to attack.

The battle of Neuve Chapelle, March

Sir Douglas Haig was in charge of the British attack. The British soldiers broke the German lines. But not for long. The

Germans sent more soldiers. The battle went on for three days. Eleven thousand British soldiers were killed or wounded.
50 Meanwhile 50,000 French were killed at Compiègne.

The second battle of Ypres

This time the Germans attacked. They wanted to try out a new weapon. It was chlorine gas. They used it against the
55 French. The French soldiers were taken by surprise.

> ‘A strange green mist, a running mass of men in agony, a 4-mile [about 6½ kilometres] gap without a defender.’
> *From B. Liddell Hart, 'Memoirs' (Cassell, 1963).*

60 The Germans seemed to be taken by surprise, too. They were slow to rush after the French. They lost their chance to break through.
    After this the British and French used
65 gas, too. But gas wasn't going to win the war. Often the wind changed direction. Then the gas blew back on the side using it.

Arras and Aubers, 9 May

The French attacked Arras. About 120,000
70 soldiers were killed or wounded.
    The British attacked at Aubers. Thousands of British soldiers climbed out of their trenches. They set off across no man's land. They were going to take the
75 German guns. They were going to drive the Germans out.
    The German soldiers sat tight in their trenches. They couldn't believe their

Gas attack on a French trench. Germany led the way in gas technology because of its advanced chemical industry. Tear gas came in January 1915, followed by the killing gases – chlorine in April 1915, phosgene in December 1915 and mustard gas in July 1917. In 1990 there will probably be about 400 men still living who were blinded by mustard gas in 1917.
    The British and French quickly followed the Germans with gas masks, gas alarms and gas.

eyes. A solid wall of soldiers came
80 towards them. The German officers shouted: 'Fire until the barrels burst.'
    The wall of soldiers crumpled. Thousands of British soldiers died.

The battle of Loos, September

Again the British attacked the Germans.
85 Again the German machine guns cut them to pieces. The battle lasted eleven days. About 60,000 British soldiers died.

The end of 1915

By the end of 1915 Britain and France were not winning the war on the Western
90 Front. Germany was not winning the war on the Western Front. Germany was also fighting Russia on the Eastern Front.
    It was going to be a long war.

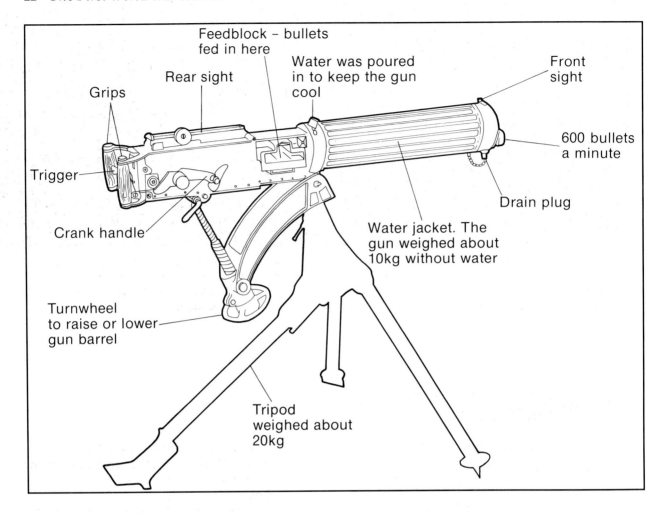

Feedblock – bullets
fed in here

Water was poured
in to keep the gun
cool

Rear sight

Front
sight

Grips

600 bullets
a minute

Trigger

Crank handle

Drain plug

Water jacket. The
gun weighed about
10kg without water

Turnwheel
to raise or lower
gun barrel

Tripod
weighed about
20kg

Look carefully at the Vickers 303 machine gun.
Then answer the following questions:

1 How was the gun kept cool?
2 Why do you think the gun got hot?
3 How many bullets did this gun fire in a
   minute?
4 How could you raise or lower the gun barrel?

There were six soldiers in a machine-gun
team. The first soldier fired the gun. The
second fed the bullets into the feedblock. The
third soldier passed bullets to number 2.
Numbers 4, 5 and 6 were fully trained reserves.
They helped carry the gun.

British troops returning from the trenches in
November 1916. Their sandbags will be full of
souvenirs to sell to soldiers behind the lines.

German barbed wire defences at Beaurevoir. This section was defended by more than fifty machine guns. It was part of the strong Hindenburg line. Soldiers had to get through the barbed wire if they needed to attack. This was no man's land. How do you think you would lay barbed wire so that your soldiers could still pass through it.

Things to Do

1 Fill in the gaps. (*Numbers in brackets refer to text line numbers.*)

It was ———— (1). The war on the ——————— (1) Front was a stalemate. The French and ——————— (3) soldiers sat in their ——————— (4). The German ——————— (4) sat in their trenches. They stared at each other across —— ———— land (6).

2 The soldiers sang many popular songs. They also made up their own words for popular tunes. The songs show the hopes and fears of the soldiers. How many ways of getting killed are mentioned in the following three songs?

Where's the old battalion?
We know where they are. We know where they are.
They're hanging on the old barbed wire.

Far, far from Ypres I long to be
Where German snipers can't get at me.
Damp is my dugout
Cold are my feet
Waiting for whizz bangs to put me to sleep.

Gassed last night
Gassed the night before
Gonna get gassed again
If we never get gassed any more.

Keywords

battalion: about 800 soldiers
sniper: someone who shoots a rifle from a hidden place
whizz bang: a light shell that whizzed along
Ypres: a much fought-over town; called Wipers by the soldiers
dugout: a shelter dug out of the side of the trench

7 The Eastern Front, 1914–17

Russia went to war in 1914. Russia was a huge country. It had a large army. The Russian king was called the tsar. He mobilized Russia's armies as quickly as
5 he could. Four armies were ready to march in ten days. The Germans were horrified. They thought the Russian armies would take six weeks to mobilize.

Moscow, August 1914

Florence Farmborough was working as a
10 nanny in Russia then.

> ❛The city was astir at an early hour and the streets were packed with excited crowds. Nicholas II, the Tsar of all the Russias, was
15 coming to visit Moscow. He was Batyushka [Little Father] to the Russian people. He was next to God. . . .❜

From Florence Farmborough, 'Nurse at the Russian Front: A Diary of 1914–18' (Constable, 1974).

Everyone was ready to fight for him and for Russia.

State of the Russian armies

The Russian armies were not ready to
20 fight. They were badly organized. For example, the whole of General Samsonov's army had only twenty-five

The Tsar blessing his soldiers.

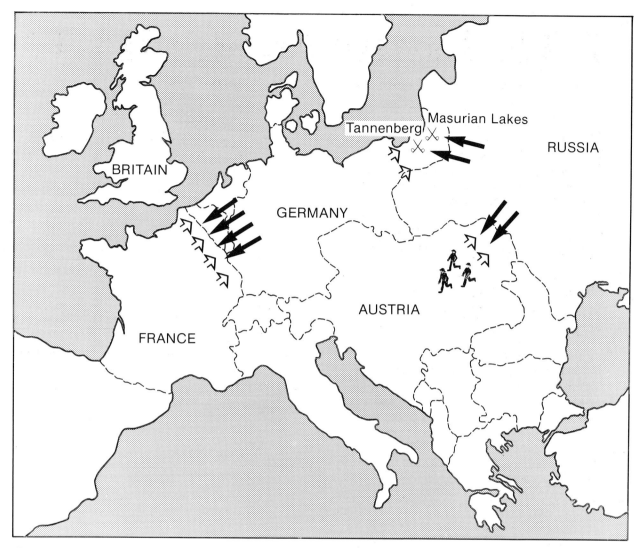

Germany fighting on the Western and Eastern Fronts.

telephones. There were not enough rifles. There were not enough boots. The radio
25 messages were not sent in code.

The Russians advance

Two Russian armies attacked Germany in the north. (Look at the map.) The Germans nearly ran away. Two German generals said no. One general was
30 Hindenburg and the other was Ludendorff. They fought back.

The battle of Tannenberg

The German army met one Russian army near Tannenberg, a village in the east of Germany. The battle lasted for five days.
35 The Russians lost 125,000 soldiers. The Germans lost 13,000 soldiers. The Russians knew they had lost. Their general was called Samsonov. He walked into a wood. He shot himself. Many
40 thousands of Russians died in the two huge lakes and in the swamps. So horrible were the screams of the drowning soldiers and horses that the Russians turned their own machine guns on them. Even so
45 movements were seen in the water for a week.

Battle of the Masurian Lakes

Then the Germans turned north. They defeated the other Russian army. The Russians were driven back.

Russia against Austria

50   But in the south it was different. The Russian armies stopped the Austrians. They drove them back. (Look at the map on page 25.) The Austrians ran away.

Russia against Turkey

55   In 1914 the Turks decided to join the war. They were on Germany's side. This was because Turkey was afraid of Russia. Turkey thought Russia wanted to take its land. So Turkey fought with Germany against Russia, France and Britain.

60   The Turks attacked Russia. But the Russians drove them back. Then it was winter time. The fighting stopped in the long, cold Russian winter. Both sides dug trenches and stayed there.

1915

65   At last spring came. The Germans joined with the Austrians. They attacked the Russians. It was a huge breakthrough for the Germans. Three quarters of a million Russian soldiers were taken prisoner.
70   Thousands and thousands died.

Florence Farmborough was now a nurse. She describes what happened on Wednesday 22 April 1915:

75   ❛ So much has happened. I am dreadfully tired. We are retreating! In that one word lies all the agony of the last few days. On Saturday the 18th explosion after explosion rent the air; our house shook, the windows rattled in their hinges. And then Death was very busy. The
80   wounded began to arrive from the Front. At first we could cope. Then they came in their hundreds. Crawling, dragging themselves. We didn't stop day and night and the noise of the

85   guns got nearer and louder. By Sunday I heard the whisper of "retreat", then louder it came and the first-line troops came into sight, dirt-bespattered, weary, desperate men. And then the order for us to retreat too. Leave everything and start without delay. We were frightened
90   and bewildered. Leave everything? Leave the wounded? But again "Skoro! skoro!" (quickly! quickly!) came the order. "The Germans are outside the town!"

Snatching up our coats and knapsacks we
95   ran down the rough road. And the wounded? They shouted to us when they saw us leaving; called out to us to take them with us; not to leave them – our brothers – to the enemy. They hopped, limped, crawled after us. All along the
100   road there were others, many others. They lay in the dust begging. We had to wrench our skirts from their clinging hands, and keep going into the night with the thunder of guns at our heels. I understood then that retreat is
105   the worst thing that can ever happen to an army.' ❜

From Florence Farmborough, 'Nurse at the Russian Front: A Diary of 1914–18'
(Constable, 1974).

Winter 1915

The winter came. The Germans had to stop. Both sides dug trenches to shelter in. The Germans were a long way from
110   home. It was a long way to bring guns and bullets and food.

In the fighting Russia had lost as much land as the whole of France. The Russians had retreated about 480 kilometres. Ten
115   million Russian people lost their homes. Many died in the cold. They retreated with the Russian army. They were refugees.

Tsar Nicholas took command

Tsar Nicholas II took command of the
120   army himself. Now he would lead the Russian people. Together they would drive the Germans out of Russia. The Russians felt strong and keen. But the Tsar was a weak man and a poor leader.
125   Russia was heading for trouble.

1916

The war was a terrible strain for Russia. The army had to have guns. The army had to be fed. So people in the towns went hungry. Factories made more guns and bullets. Russian factories made 10,000 rifles a month. The Russian soldiers had more guns than they had early in the war. But could they defeat the Germans?

The Russians attack the Germans

The Russians attacked the Germans. It was a disaster for the Russians. The Germans knew their plans. They shot the Russians to pieces. Five Russian soldiers died for every one German.

The Brusilov attack

Brusilov was a Russian general in the south. He took a risk. He attacked the Austrians there. By October 1916 he was deep into Austria. The Austrian army was collapsing. Then the Germans helped the Austrians. They helped by attacking Russia's ally Rumania. Quickly the Germans defeated Rumania.

Winter 1916–17

The war had lasted for more than two years. The Russians had not lost the war, but they had not won either.

The German generals, Hindenburg and Ludendorff.

Russian Cossack soldiers.

Things to Do

1 Fill in the gaps. (*Numbers in brackets refer to text line numbers.*)

————— (1) went to war in 1914. It had a large ——— (2). The Russian king was called the ——— (3). He mobilized Russia's ————— (4) as quickly as he could.

2 Read the following paragraphs. Then answer the questions.

‘The Grand Duke stated that he had to stop fighting because he had no ammunition and no boots for his soldiers.’

From 'Memoirs of M. Rodzianko', 1927.

‘There is plenty of meat in Siberia but we cannot get it here. We need 300 locomotives to pull the trains to bring it here. We haven't got them.’

General Gurko

(a) Write down the three things that the soldiers did not have.

(b) Why did the soldiers have no meat?

3 Look at the word square. Copy it into your book. In the word square are some of the important words. The words can run in any direction. Cross them out as you find them. You should find:

Russia	boots
Nicholas	Austria
Tannenberg	Moscow
tsar	Masurian
Hindenburg	Lakes
Brusilov	code

Which Russian general is missing?

R	U	S	S	I	A	W	X	N	T
B	M	A	A	U	S	T	R	I	A
R	A	M	O	S	C	O	W	C	N
U	S	S	F	L	Z	P	Y	H	N
S	U	O	B	F	A	N	B	O	E
I	R	N	G	O	C	K	L	L	N
L	I	O	H	C	O	J	E	A	B
O	A	V	S	O	L	T	Z	S	E
V	N	E	Q	D	Q	T	S	A	R
H	I	N	D	E	N	B	U	R	G

8 War in the Air

It was 1914. Aeroplanes were 11 years old. That was all. Would aeroplanes be useful in the war? Nobody knew. All the great countries had some aeroplanes.

5 Aeroplanes were useful for seeing. A pilot saw a great deal from an aeroplane or a balloon. So it was difficult to keep a secret. Each side wanted to get rid of the aeroplanes belonging to the other side. At

10 first the pilots had pistols. They shot at each other. Then they had machine guns. Soon special fighter aeroplanes were made.

The Fokker aeroplane 1915

Fokker was an inventor. He invented a
15 cam-operated synchronizing gear. This meant that the gun stopped firing when the airscrew blades passed in front of the gun. The synchronizing gear worked. A German Fokker plane followed a British
20 plane. The German plane fired quickly and easily straight ahead. The machine-gun bullets hit the British plane in the tail. Time after time the German Fokker planes shot down British and French
25 planes.

The Fokker Eindecker (monoplane) had a maximum speed of 87.5 m.p.h. The light wings warped in the air and this caused many crashes, so aeroplane makers went back to making biplanes.

Wicker-work pilot's seat, light but strong

Pylon for landing wires. The wires helped to give the wings strength

Welded steel tube fuselage frame

Extra fuel tank

New synchronised machine gun

Wooden fin and elevator

Laminated wooden airscrew

Tail skid sprung with thick rubber

Linen covering, This was stretched tight, painted with cellulose dope. The dope made the linen shrink. It made it waterproof

9-cylinder 100 horse-power engine

Front fuel tank

Main spar

Undercarriage (sprung on thick rubber cord) and anchorage point for main flying wires

Leather strengthening strips

Ribs

Wire spoked wheels (covered in)

Max Immelmann – a German air ace

Max Immelmann was born in 1890. He joined the Germany army when he grew up. He loved engines. War started in 1914. He joined the *Fliegertruppe*. He learnt to
30   fly.

1 August 1915

Immelmann woke up suddenly. Engines were roaring. He heard the loud crump of bombs. Ten British planes were bombing the Doberitz airfield. The German pilots
35   leapt out of bed. They pulled on their goggles. They threw on their jackets over their nightshirts.
   Immelmann jumped into the nearest plane. It was a Fokker E111. Immelmann
40   had never flown a plane like it. In minutes he was in the air. The British planes had gone. But Immelmann chased them. He roared up behind a slow British plane. He fired sixty rounds of bullets. Then his
45   machine gun jammed. But the British plane was spinning to the ground. Immelmann turned for home. He was given a medal, the Iron Cross.
   He carried on fighting. He shot down
50   fifteen British and French planes. Then in June 1916 Immelmann was shot down. He was dead.

Air fighting between German and British planes. Fighting an enemy aeroplane if you met one in the sky was almost inevitable. But some people said it was just widening the area in which men fought and was not *winning the war. Apart from fighting other aeroplanes what jobs did pilots and observers do to help win the war?*

Two observers checking their Lewis guns in the Squadron's Armoury in France, 1918. What does the clothing of the observers tell you about conditions in the air?

Summer 1916

Air fighting was changing. The British had better planes now. They had the DH2
55 and the FE26.

Uses of aeroplanes

It was 1916. Everyone knew that aeroplanes were useful in war. Observers in planes saw what the enemy was doing. Fighter planes shot down the observer's
60 aeroplanes and balloons. Aeroplanes also did ground strafing. This means they shot at soldiers from the air. Also bombs were dropped from aeroplanes.
   Now there was war in the air as well as
65 on land and sea.

1916–17

The Germans made new and better planes. It was 1917. The Germans controlled the sky over the Western Front. The French and British called
70 April 'Bloody April'. The British lost 316 aircrew. The Germans lost 114 aircrew.

The pilots

The pilots were young. Most of them did not live long. In April 1917 a pilot on the Western Front was expected to live three
75 weeks.

What made a good pilot?

All the pilots of France, Germany, Britain, Austria, Italy, Russia and the USA were brave, keen and loved excitement. The outstanding pilots were
80 good shots and natural fliers. René Fonck was a French air ace. He said: 'To do well you must know how to control your nerves.' Fonck shot down seventy-five German planes by the end of the war. He
85 was 24 years old then.

An Australian crew in 1917. How do you know they are about to take off? How many machine guns are carried? The writing on the gunner's cockpit says: 'Do not fly with less than 150 lb [68.4 kg] in the gunner's compartment.' Why do you think this is written here? Do you think the pilot's machine gun is synchronised or not (see the section on the Fokker aeroplane 1915)?

Air fighting

Between 1914 and 1916 the pilots fought alone. They stalked each other. They attacked out of the clouds with the sun behind them.

90 After 1916 Germany, France and Britain had more planes. The planes were faster. They had more guns. Pilots were trained to fly in formation. This means lots of planes flying together.

1918

95 The war had lasted four years. Germany did not have enough steel. It did not have enough oil. It could not make enough aeroplanes. It did not have enough pilots. Germany did not have enough fuel. It was
100 August 1918. Each aeroplane was allowed only 150 litres of fuel a day.

France and Britain had enough aeroplanes. The USA had joined the war on their side.

105 The German pilots fought to the end. It was 11 November 1918. The war was over. The Germans had lost. In a few months' time they had to give up 2,000 aeroplanes. They burnt some. They flew some to
110 France. They broke some up.

Things to Do

1 Fill in the gaps. (*Numbers in brackets refer to text line numbers.*)
It was –––– (1). Aeroplanes were –– (1) years old. A pilot saw a great deal from an aeroplane or a –––––– (7). Each side wanted to get rid of the –––––––––– (9) belonging to the other side.

2 Read the section headed 'Uses of aeroplanes'. Make a list of all the ways in which aeroplanes were useful in the war.

3 Write a heading in your exercise book: 'What made a good pilot'. Choose words from the list below that you think describe a good pilot?'

slow good eyesight careful
brave keen   hates excitement
careless a good shot natural flier

4 Pilots became very fond of the planes they flew. The following is a verse from an airforce song:

There are finer machines, with much
 better windscreens,
And whose pilots don't know what a dud
 engine means,
But my good old Avro can loop, roll or
 spin,
And there isn't a field that I can't put
 her in.

(a) What do you think a dud engine means to a pilot?

(b) What can his Avro do? Why do you think this may be useful?

(c) What does the last line mean? Why could this be very useful?

Photographs of Passchendaele taken from an aeroplane before and after the battle. You can see the streets and the town in the left-hand

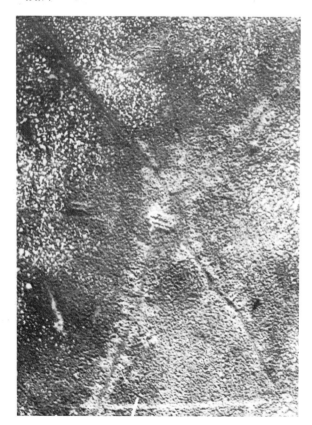

photo. What other things would pilots be very keen to photograph from the air during the war?

9 The Attack on the Dardanelles

It was 1915. On the Western Front the French and British armies faced the German armies. Both sides lived in trenches. They shot at each other. No one was winning. No one was even moving.

5 Some people said that the war might go on for ever. David Lloyd George was a member of the British War Council. He wrote:

10 ❝ Germany and Austria have between them 3 million young men ready to take the place of the men now in the trenches when these fall. I frankly despair that we can ever win. ❞

A new idea

Winston Churchill was the First Lord of
15 the Admiralty. He suggested attacking Turkey. Turkey was on the side of Germany.

The British and French agreed to attack Turkey. They wanted to knock Turkey out of the war. Then they could send help to Russia.

They could send ships into the Black Sea. They could also attack Austria and Germany from the Dardanelles.

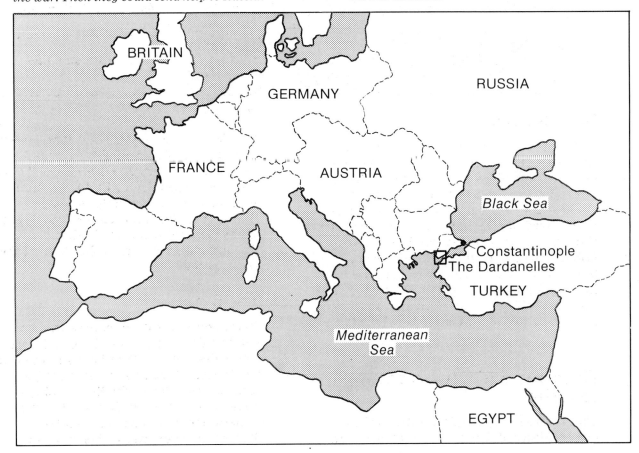

BRITAIN
GERMANY
RUSSIA
FRANCE
AUSTRIA
Black Sea
Constantinople
The Dardanelles
TURKEY
Mediterranean Sea
EGYPT

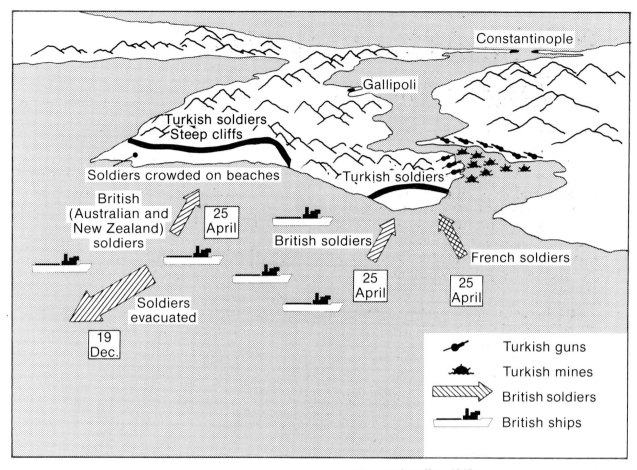

The following labels appear on the map:

- Constantinople
- Gallipoli
- Turkish soldiers
- Steep cliffs
- Soldiers crowded on beaches
- Turkish soldiers
- British (Australian and New Zealand) soldiers
- 25 April
- British soldiers
- French soldiers
- 25 April
- 25 April
- Soldiers evacuated
- 19 Dec.

Legend:
- Turkish guns
- Turkish mines
- British soldiers
- British ships

March 1915

At first the British ships tried to force their way through the Dardanelles (look at the maps). They had to do two things. They had to destroy the Turkish guns. These guns were on the hills on each side of the Dardanelles. They also had to clear the mines from the Dardanelles. They failed. Three British battleships were blown up by the mines. Corporal Tom Eades said it was terrifying. He wrote in his diary: 'We are threading our way through miles of mines floating like large corks.'

The army and navy work together

There were many soldiers stationed in Egypt. Many of them were Australian and

The Dardanelles, 1915.

New Zealand soldiers. They were known as ANZAC soldiers. ANZAC stands for Australia and New Zealand Army Corps. They were fighting for Britain. These soldiers were sent to help take the Dardanelles from the Turks. They were led by General Hamilton. Admiral Robeck was in charge of the ships at the Dardanelles.

The plan

Hamilton and Robeck planned to land soldiers on the beaches. These soldiers would destroy the Turkish guns and take the Dardanelles. The mines would be cleared away. Then the British ships could sail through to Constantinople. Constantinople was the capital of Turkey. Turkey would then give up.

Turkish gun battery at the entrance to the Dardanelles.

Gallipoli

50 The beaches were at a place called
Gallipoli. Nobody had made good plans.
Nobody had worked out exactly how the
soldiers would rush up the cliffs to take
the Turkish guns. For example, Hamilton
55 had no good maps of the Gallipoli
peninsula. He stayed on board his ship
well away from the fighting.

The Turks

German officers led the Turkish army.
General von Sanders was put in charge on
60 26 March. He had a grim job. The Turkish
soldiers were ragged and weak. How could
these poor soldiers fight off the British?
    The Turkish soldiers were spread thinly
along the bare brown cliffs. They did not
65 have many guns. They had no aeroplanes.
They knew the British were going to
attack. So they waited.

Things to Do

1 Fill in the gaps. (*Numbers in brackets*
refer to text line numbers.)
It was ---- (1). Some people said that
the war might go on for ---- (7).
Winston --------- (14) was the First
Lord of the Admiralty. He suggested
attacking ------ (16). Turkey was on
the side of ------- (17).

2 Read the section headed 'March 1915'.
Then write out the paragraph below.
Choose the correct word from the
brackets.
At first the (Bulgarian/British) ships tried
to force their way through the (dishes/
Dardanelles/drains). They had to do
(two/five) things. They had to destroy the
Turkish (ghosts/gums/guns). They also
had to clear the (mines/mice) from the
Dardanelles. They (failed/succeeded).

3 General Hamilton was in charge of all the
British soldiers. Lieutenant-General
Birdwood worked for him. In 1915

Lieutenant-General Birdwood said about General Hamilton:

> 'Hamilton should have really taken command and told us what to do. He has never done that yet.'

Choose a word from the list below which you think best describes how Lieutenant-General Birdwood felt about Hamilton.

pleased	uncaring
confident	angry
bitter	sad

4 Sir M. Hankey was a member of Britain's War Council. He wrote:

> 'No one has worked out how many soldiers and guns are needed to take Gallipoli from the Turks. We have just said that we can ship a certain number of soldiers there and that ought to be enough.'

Talk in class about what the writer is saying. Discuss what advantages and disadvantages each side had by the time the British landed at Gallipoli.

5 Do the crossword. (*Numbers in brackets after clues refer to text line numbers. You will need to read the whole sentence to find the answer.*)

ACROSS

1 The beaches were at a place called —————————. (50)
4 Admiral —————— was in charge of the ships at the Dardanelles. (39)
9 'We are threading——— way through miles of mines floating like large corks.' (28)
10 He had a ———— job. (60)
11 'Germany and Austria have between them 3 million young men ready to take the place of the men ——— in the trenches when these fall.' (10)
12 He stayed on board his ship ———— away from the fighting. (56)
15 —— they waited. (67)
16 These soldiers were sent to help take the Dardanelles from the ——————. (36)

DOWN

1 On the Western Front the French and British armies faced the —————— armies. (1)
2 Some people said that the war might go—— for ever. (6)
3 Both sides lived—— trenches. (3)
5 Three British battleships were ————— up by the mines. (25)
6 'We are threading our way through miles of mines floating like large —————.' (28)
7 'We are threading our way through miles of mines floating like ————— corks.' (28)
8 They were led by General —————————. (38)
12 The Turkish soldiers were ragged and ————. (60)
13 German officers ——— the Turkish army. (58)
14 They did ——— have many guns. (64)

10 Fighting on the Gallipoli Peninsula

Landing at Anzac Cove, 25 April 1915

A New Zealand soldier wrote in his diary on 28 April:

'First chance of scribbling anything for three days. Been through hell – just that!

It was dark when our boat left the ship and crept towards the denser blackness of the shore. Not a light twinkled ahead. Not a sound. Had we taken the Turks by surprise? Or were they lying low waiting? On the boats crept as the sky got brighter. It was red now over the dim hills ahead. Then we were close to land. We heard the "wouff" of waves breaking on the sand. Behind us the big, grey British battleships sat like silent watchdogs in the early morning haze. Ahead we saw the curving beach and the cliffs all of 400 feet [about 120 metres] high. And all the time it grew lighter – a lovely quiet summer day at the sea.

Were there any Turks? God were they never going to show themselves?

Crash, bang, zzzzzip. It was hell let loose. The whole beach went up in flames in front of us. Bullets hit us like a blizzard of lead. The boat next to ours was torn apart – bodies, blood, splinters of wood. Bodies jammed so tight in other small boats they couldn't even fall over. We were stunned. For a second the whole sea of boats faltered. Then suddenly out dived the soldiers, bayonets fixed, yelling up the beach, throwing off the heavy packs, straight into the Turkish guns. I've never seen such brave men. Nothing could have stopped them.'

From 'On the Anzac Trail'
(the diary of a New Zealand soldier).

Soldiers landing at Anzac Cove.

*Look carefully. A Turkish sniper captured by
two Australian soldiers.*

The Turks

35 Thousands of soldiers landed on the
beach. Only one big gun was landed that
day. These British, New Zealand,
Australian and French soldiers were
invading Turkey. The Turkish soldiers
fought hard. A young colonel called
40 Mustapha Kemal encouraged them. By
night-time the Turks had pushed the
British soldiers back. The soldiers were
huddled on the beach. The widest part of
the beach was about 1 kilometre.

The trenches

45 The days passed. The soldiers were told to
dig trenches. And there they sat day in,
day out. It was cold at night and hot in
the day. There were dust, and flies and
very little water. The soldiers were
50 trapped on the beaches and on the lower
part of the cliffs.

> 6 The hillsides are honeycombed with dugouts
and the cliff face looks quite pretty at night
with hundreds of twinkling lights (candles)
55 showing clearly. There are few doors to the
men's dugouts. 9

*From 'The War Diary and Letters of Corporal
Tom Eades, 1915–17'
(Cambridge Aids to Learning, 1972).*

In the day the summer sun beat down on
all the soldiers. Every scrap of food, water,
bullets, spades, barbed wire, bandages
60 and so on, had to be brought by ships.

> 6 At nine o'clock we were paraded and the
Commander of Anzac addressed us. We learnt
that we were to do the unloading of supply
ships on the beach. We shall always be
65 unloading under fire and without the shelter of
the trenches so this is going to be a hell of a
place for us. 9

*From 'The War Diary of Corporal Tom Eades,
1915–17' (Cambridge Aids to Learning, 1972).*

24 May 1915

Every time there was fighting on the
hillside bodies piled up. It was so hot they
70 went bad very quickly. Both sides were
keen to bury their dead.

> 6 We had the truce yesterday. I was afraid
something might go wrong but it all went off
all right. At 7.30 we met the Turks, Miralai
75 Izzedin, a pleasant, rather sharp little man, and
Arif, the son of Achmet Pasha. We walked
from the sea and uphill through a field of tall
corn, filled with poppies, through another
field, then the fearful smell of death began as
80 we came upon scattered bodies. We came
over the top of a hill and 4,000 Turkish bodies
lay among the thyme and myrtle. It was a
nightmare. A Turkish soldier gave me some
antiseptic wool with scent on it to cover my
85 nose. There were two wounded crying in the
mountains of dead nearby. The Turkish
captain turned to me. "God pity all us poor
soldiers," was all he said. 9

*From A. Herbert, 'Locusts of Steel' in
'The Great War – I Was There', vol. 1 1914–16.*

Things to Do

1 Fill in the gaps. (*Numbers in brackets refer to text line numbers.*)
   Thousands of –––––––– (34) landed on the beach. These –––––––– (36), New Zealand, Australian and –––––– (37) soldiers were invading Turkey. The –––––––– (38) soldiers fought hard. By night-time the Turks had pushed the –––––––– (42) soldiers back. The days passed. The soldiers were told to dig –––––––– (46).

2 Read the section headed 'The landing at Anzac Cove, 25 April 1915'. Then answer the questions:
   (a) Who wrote the diary?
   (b) What does the writer say he has been through?
   (c) How did he know that his boat was getting near to land?
   (d) How high were the cliffs?
   (e) Choose the word that the writer uses to describe his fellow soldiers from the list below:

scared	terrified
worried	calm
foolhardy	stupid
confident	happy
brave	relaxed
excited	gentle

   Then imagine you are one of the soldiers rushing up the beach. Choose one other word to describe how you might feel. Discuss your choice in class.

3 Read the section headed 'The trenches'. Then answer the questions:
   (a) Where did the soldiers build dugouts?
   (b) Did they have electricity?
   (c) Why could you see the lights?
   (d) What job was Tom Eades given?
   (e) What makes him think that the place will be like hell?

5 Read the section headed '24 May 1915'. Then answer the questions:
   (a) Why did the Turkish soldier give Herbert antiseptic wool?
   (b) What did the Turkish captain say?
   (c) What is a truce?

6 Read the letter below in class. How many mistakes can you find?

Dear Mum,
   We landed on the beach at Gallipoli in the evening. It was raining so the Turks could not see us. We jumped out of the boats and strolled up the beach. Now we are all living safely in tents on top of the cliffs. Many flowers grow here and they look lovely, but the Turks are very savage. They do not even look after their own wounded. There are flies and dust everywhere, but thank heavens we have plenty of water.
   With love from
   Ken

11 Suvla Bay – the End of Gallipoli

It was 6 August. The British decided to attack the Turks again. This time they were going to drive the Turks back from the top of the cliffs. The Anzac soldiers attacked from their beach. Meanwhile 20,000 British and Indian soldiers landed at Suvla Bay. Only 1,000 Turks faced them. The Turks were desperate. But the British General told his soldiers to stay on the beach. They could attack the Turks later. He had an afternoon sleep. Two days later he told the soldiers to attack the Turks. Secretly the Turks had brought in thousands of soldiers. They were ready. They shot the British soldiers to pieces. The Anzac soldiers were driven back, too. It was a disaster for the British.

Both sides tunnelled. They wanted to blow up each other's trenches. They could hear each other digging. They would stop to listen. It was a race to get as near to the enemy trench as possible, then blow it up before you were blown up.

The end of the Gallipoli campaign

All the landings and attacks had been badly organized. Thousands of soldiers had died. Australians, New Zealanders,

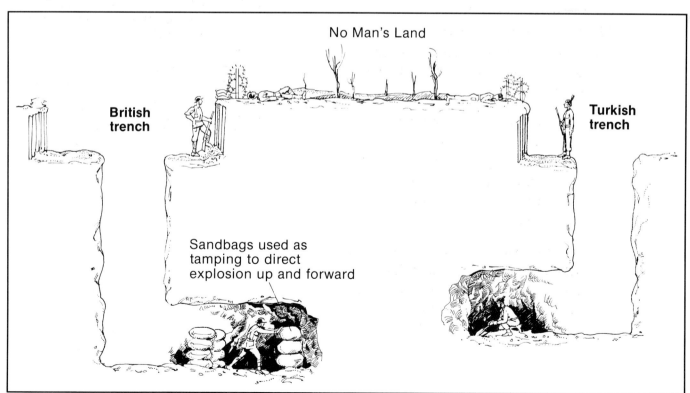

No Man's Land

British trench

Turkish trench

Sandbags used as tamping to direct explosion up and forward

Indians, British and French soldiers had died.

25   It was 19 December 1915. Everyone knew that the British had not won.

General Hamilton was sacked. General Monro took his place. He decided to evacuate the Anzac and British soldiers from Gallipoli.'Hooray,' wrote Tom

30   Eades. 'Six hours' notice to leave this cursed spot!' The evacuation was well organized. Not a single soldier died.

The British getting ready to leave 'W' beach, Suvla Bay, January 1916.

The government

In Britain people were shocked. They turned on the government. Winston

35   Churchill was sacked. The Liberal government fell. The Liberal and Conservative parties joined together to form a government. A government that is made up of two or more parties is called

40   a coalition.

Results of Gallipoli

1 200,000 Australian, New Zealand, British and French soldiers were killed or wounded.
2 Probably more Turkish soldiers were killed and wounded.
3 The Dardanelles remained closed so no supplies could get to Russia from Britain and France.
4 Turkey stayed on Germany's side.
5 British people were horrified by the number of soldiers who were lost at Gallipoli.
6 The Government decided to concentrate on the Western Front. It said that was where the war would be won or lost.

Things to Do

1 Fill in the gaps. (*Numbers in brackets refer to text line numbers.*)

It was 6 —————— (1). The British decided to attack the ————— (2) again. The ————— (4) soldiers attacked from their beach. Meanwhile 20,000 British and —————— (6) soldiers landed at ————— (7) Bay. It was disaster for the ——————— (18).

2 A young British miner from Durham was a soldier at Gallipoli:

'I went for a swim in the bay. Lovely day. Just had to look out for shells whizzing over. I decided to swim out to one of the ship's and beg some bread as it was so long since we had any. I was getting near when suddenly I felt a bang through the water that lifted me clean up and turned me round so I was swimming the opposite way. By the time I'd turned back I couldn't believe my eyes. The ship I'd been swimming to was on her side with hundreds of sailors jumping overboard. In another few minutes she'd sunk. So much for my loaf of bread.'

From J. Murray, 'Gallipoli As I Saw It'.

Corporal Tom Eades wrote in his diary in August:

'At dusk the rifle bullets fell thickly and we laid in our hole listening. The Turks are no more than 200 yards [about 180 metres] away. Some of our group have been digging new trenches further back, but we prefer our cliff hideout. The new trenches are too low down. More men get killed on the beaches than tucked up in the cliffs. Salt beef today, hard biscuit and only one pint of tea for drink all day. Kept the bottom half inch for shaving water.'

*From 'The War Diary and Letters of Tom Eades, 1915–17'
(Cambridge Aids to Learning, 1972).*

You are a soldier coming home from Gallipoli. All the letters you sent to your family while you were in Gallipoli have been seen by the censor. (Censors read all letters written by soldiers. They were looking for anything that could help the enemy. Even information about where a soldier was could help the enemy. The censors cut out this kind of information from letters.) So you have not been able to tell your family much about Gallipoli. Now, sitting on board a ship coming home you decide to write a brief account of what it was like. Mention the landing at Anzac Cove, the cliffs and beaches, the trenches, the weather, the food and the swimming.

12 War at Sea

Britain owned many other countries in the world. Britain needed ships. It needed to sail to the countries it owned. Britain needed to trade with many countries.

5   Germany was a great country. It wanted to own other countries, too. It built a huge navy. But it was difficult for Germany to use it. (Look at the map below).

Britain is an island. It had many ships. They could sail anywhere in the world. They carried soldiers to France. They brought soldiers from India, Australia and Canada. They brought food to Britain. Why do you think it was more difficult for Germany to sail its ships to other countries?

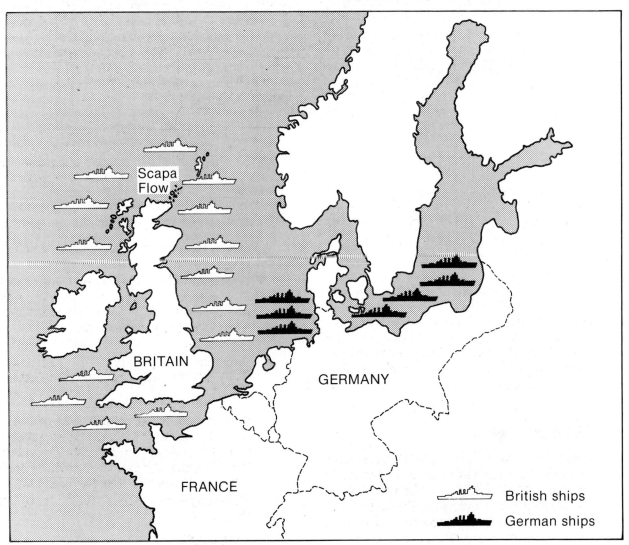

Scapa Flow

BRITAIN

GERMANY

FRANCE

⌐═▦═ British ships
▬▰▬ German ships

The Emden *was a successful German raider. It sank many British ships before it was wrecked. The* Emden *had a false funnel which could be raised or lowered. Why do you think this was useful to the German ship?*

1914

10 Many huge British ships were based at Scapa Flow. The British did not need to attack the German fleet. They just had to stop German ships coming out of port. Then British ships could come and go as 15 they pleased.

But the German ships had to get out. They wanted to stop food and guns reaching Britain. They needed to sink British ships. Some German ships stayed 20 outside of their ports. These were raiders. They raided and sank British ships all over the world.

1916

Two things changed in 1916. First, it was obvious that the war was a stalemate. No 25 one was winning on land. Perhaps the Germans could win at sea. Secondly, Admiral Scheer was made commander-in-chief of the German High Seas Fleet. He

30 wanted to fight the British. He wanted to win.

The British wanted to win, too. Perhaps they could win at sea. So the British were keen to fight. Admiral Jellicoe was in charge of the British ships.

The battle of Jutland, May 1916

35 Scheer decided to fight it out with the British. The British knew that Scheer meant to attack. This was because the British knew the German radio code.

It was afternoon. The British fleet 40 picked up a radio signal from the German ships:

31GG2490

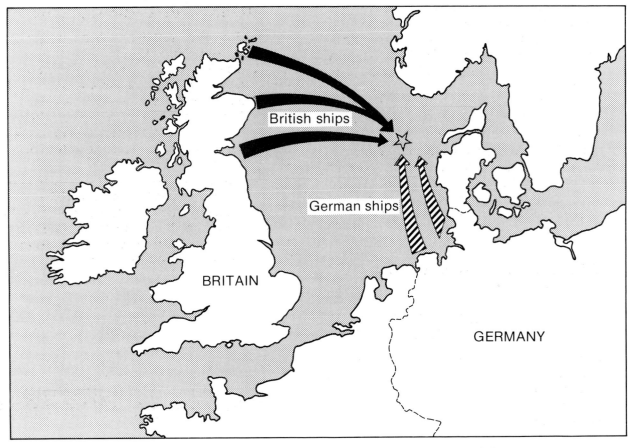

The battle of Jutland, 1916.

This meant '**Carry out secret instruction 2490 on 31 May**'.

45   The British did not know what 2490 was. But they knew the Germans were up to something. The British Grand Fleet sailed out from Scapa Flow. The ships stretched out for 26 kilometres across the

50   sea. At the same time the German High Seas Fleet sailed into the North Sea.

Jutland

The two fleets met at Jutland. Through the summer afternoon and evening the great ships fired their huge guns. There

55   were flashes of orange fire in the thick smoke. The ships turned. They chased each other. They covered kilometres of sea.

This is a rare action photograph of the battle of Jutland. It was taken from a British destroyer. It shows HMS Lion *on fire. Why do you think there are very few, clear photographs of the battle?*

60 The German guns were smaller. But the armour on German ships was thicker. The German ships did not sink so easily. Soon three British ships were hit. Then another British ship, the *Indefatigable*, was sunk.
65 Then the *Queen Mary* was blown up. It sank with the propellers still turning.

But by this time all the British ships had arrived. Several German ships were sunk. Now the Germans faced a really huge British fleet. Scheer decided to head
70 for home. With luck and clever sailing he got away. The German ships disappeared in the darkness. The battle of Jutland was over.

What each side lost at the battle of Jutland

	British	German
75 Battle cruisers	3	1
Armoured cruisers	3	0
Old battle 80 ships	0	1
Light cruisers	0	4
Destroyers	8	5
Weight of all 85 ships sunk	113,800 tonnes	62,000 tonnes
Sailors killed	6,000	2,500

Results of the battle of Jutland

1 Both the British and German fleets were still strong.
2 The German fleet stayed at home for
90 most of the rest of the war. It did not dare come out again.
3 The British had to keep a very large fleet of ships. These ships had to make sure that the German fleet stayed
95 bottled up.
4 The Germans decided that they could not defeat the British fleet. They decided to use submarines to stop ships taking food to Britain. This almost
100 worked. But it brought the USA into the war against Germany.

Things to Do

1 Fill in the gaps. (*Numbers in brackets refer to text line numbers.*)
Britain ––––– (1) many other countries in the world. It needed to –––– (3) to the countries it owned. German ships wanted to stop –––– (17) and –––– (17) reaching ––––––– (18).

2 Look at the table showing what each side lost at the battle of Jutland (lines 74–86). Then answer the following questions:
(a) How many ships did the British lose?
(b) How many ships did the Germans lose?
(c) Who lost the greatest weight of ships?
(d) Who lost most sailors?
(e) Who do you think won the battle of Jutland?

Page from the Jutland despatches.

Date, time of despatch	From	To	System	Message	Time of origin
1 JUNE 8.10 a.m.	Admiralty	Captain S., Maidstone	W/T	Recall *Firedrake* and her group of submarines.	0810
8.10	Commodore F.	Destroyers	Flags	Alter course in succession to E.N.E.	—
8.10	*S.O. B.C.F.*	*S.O. 1st B.C.S.*	Sem.	Can you throw any light as to destruction of *Queen Mary*? Reply: It appeared to be an explosion in *Queen Mary's* magazine due to a salvo hitting.	0809
8.12	S.O. B.C.F.	S.O. 2nd B.C.S.	Sem.	Can you throw any light as to the cause of destruction of *Indefatigable*? Reply: Salvo struck her aft and apparently explosion reached magazine.	0810
8.12	S.O. 4th L.C.S.	4th L.C.S.	Flags	Zigzag 1½ points. First turn to starboard. Admiral intends to proceed 17½ knots.	—
8.14	Captain D13	S.O. B.C.F.	W/T	My position, course and speed at 8 a.m. 56° 42′ N., 5° 47′ E., South, 20 knots. Request instructions.	0800
				Reply: Collect your flotilla and rejoin.	0828
8.15	*Benbow*	—	—	Remarks: Passed a large quantity of oil and a cork lifebuoy.	—
8.15	*Benbow*	C.-in-C.	Flags	Mine in sight.	—
8.16	*Biarritz*	Lowestoft	W/T	A trawler has just held me up in middle ocean. Is Channel clear? Reply: Channel is clear.	0740
8.17	*Princess Royal*	*Lion*	Sem.	Comdr. N. to ditto. At 7.15 a.m. using Lat. 55° 26′ N., Long. 6° 29½ E., obtained intercepts 1¾ miles N. 82 W. Reply: Thank you, I had similar results.	0745
8.20	Admiralty	Captain S., Maidstone	W/T	Send four fresh submarines for seven-day period to same stations off Dutch coast as last week. Not to be done by wireless.	0820
				Reply: Propose to send Submarine E.41 as one of the four submarines if not required for mine-laying.	1008
8.20	*Warspite*	S.O. 5th B.S.	W/T	Position Lat. 56° 39′ N., Long. 1° 43′ E., course W., speed of advance 16 knots. Condition: Many holes from shell fire, several through armour and below water line, wing engine room practically tight with bulkhead shored, several compartments full, ship on even keel, steering from engine room. *(Passed to C.-in-C.)*	0610
8.20	*Badger*	S.O. B.C.F.	Sem.	Oil remaining at 8 a.m.:　　　Tons 　*Badger*　　　72 　*Acheron*　　70 　*Ariel*　　　76 　*Attack*　　　60 　*Hydra*　　　77 　*Lizard*　　　56 　*Goshawk*　　74 　*Lapwing*　　74	—
8.22	S.O. 5th B.S.	5th B.S.	Flags	Alter course together two points to port.	—
8.23	C.-in-C.	*Marksman*, S.O. B.C.F.	W/T	My position at 8.15 a.m., 55° 54′ N., 6° 10′ E. What will your position be at 8.15 a.m.?	0800
8.24	C.-in-C.	*Dublin*	S.L.	Close	—

3 Look at the page from the Jutland
   despatches opposite.

   Key
   S.O.   Senior Officer
   B.C.F.   Battle Cruiser Fleet
   B.C.S.   Battle Cruiser Squadron
   L.C.S.   Light Cruiser Squadron
   C-in-C   Comander-in-Chief
   B.S.   Battle Squadron

   (a) What is the date of these entries?
   (b) How many messages are recorded?
   (c) At what time was the first message
       sent?
   (d) At what time was the last message
       sent?
   (e) How many different ways of sending
       messages are there? (Talk about what
       they mean in class.)

   (f) Look at the message sent at 8.20 a.m.
       from the Admiralty (in London) to
       Maidstone. Why do you think the
       order about the submarines must not
       be sent by wireless (radio)?
   (g) Look at the message at 8.20 a.m. from
       Badger (a destroyer) to the Senior
       Officer of the Battle Cruiser Fleet.
       What fuel did the destroyers use?
       Why do you think it was important for
       the Senior Officer to know how much
       fuel each destroyer had left?
   (h) Who was the Commander-in-Chief of
       the British fleet at the battle of
       Jutland (line 33)?

13 Verdun, 1916

The Germans were holding their line of trenches on the Western Front. Slowly, they were defeating the Russians on the Eastern Front. So Germany did not need as many soldiers on the Eastern Front. It sent half a million soldiers across to the Western Front. This was bad news for the French and British.

General Falkenhayn

General Falkenhayn was in charge of the German soldiers. The Germans were not doing badly. But they still had to beat the French and British. Then they could win the war. Falkenhayn decided to attack the French fortress of Verdun. This would stop the French and British attacking the Germans.

The French were very proud of Verdun. It was a great fortress. French people did not know that the guns had been taken away. They had been sent to help the war in other places. So Verdun was an empty shell. But Falkenhayn knew that the French would not let Verdun go.

'Bleed the French white'

Falkenhayn decided to use thousands of German soldiers. He wanted to make the French fight at Verdun. He wanted the French army to lose all its soldiers. Falkenhayn would bleed the French army white.

Germany defeated Russia. Germany was no longer fighting on the Eastern Front. Germany sent half a million soldiers to the Western Front.

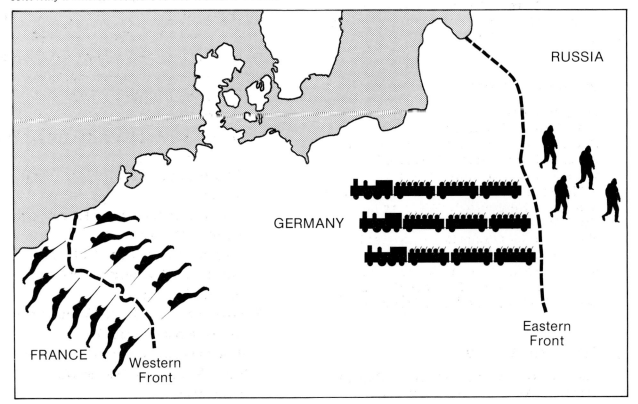

Ruined houses in a suburb of Verdun.

February 1916

30 The Germans put 1,400 guns on the hills around Verdun. On 21 February they started to fire. Two million shells pounded Verdun. Then the Germans rushed in to attack. After three days the
35 Germans were about to take Verdun.

Why hold Verdun?

Many important French soldiers said that Verdun did not matter. If the Germans won Verdun they would have got one old useless fort. That's all. It
40 would not help them win the war.

The French Prime Minister was angry and upset. He shouted: 'You may not think Verdun is important but everyone else in France thinks it is important.'
45 General Pétain was told to save Verdun. He was firm and hopeful. He said: 'Ils ne passeront pas [They shall not pass].' The French soldiers fought on.

The Sacred Way

There was one way into Verdun. Day and
50 night trucks drove along this 'Sacred Way'. They carried soldiers, food, bullets, shells, medicine and guns. They kept Verdun alive.

July 1916

Verdun was bleeding France white. But it
55 was bleeding Germany white, too. It was July 1916. The Germans gave up the battle for Verdun. The French had saved Verdun.

The battle of the Somme

The British promised to help the French.
60 The British attacked the Germans. This was the battle of the Somme.

Things to Do

1 Fill in the gaps. (*Numbers in brackets refer to text line numbers.*)
   The Germans were holding their line of ———————— (2) on the ———————— (2) Front. Slowly, ———— (3) were defeating the ———————— (3) on the Eastern Front. So Germany did not need as many soldiers on the Eastern Front. It sent half a ———————— (6) soldiers across to the Western ———— (7).
2 Who was put in charge of the German soldiers?
3 What French fortress did Falkenhayn decide to attack?
4 Read the section headed 'Bleed the French white'. What does 'bleed the French white' mean?
5 How many guns did the Germans put on the hills around Verdun?
6 Read the section headed 'The Sacred Way'. Why was the Sacred Way important?

14 The Battle of the Somme, 1916

24 June–1 July

The British guns pounded the German trenches. The big guns blazed for seven days.

5 ❛While the guns were blazing when we saw what was happening to the German front trenches, we all had our tails up. We thought nothing could survive that bombardment.❜

Bill Partridge, 7th Middlesex, in a TV documentary.

A 15-inch Howitzer being prepared for action, July 1916. The 15 inches [38 cm] refers to the diameter of the barrel. A Howitzer is a gun with a barrel that can be raised. This means that it can fire at targets over a hill without hitting the hill.

10 The British guns stood almost side by side for 29 kilometres. People could hear the thunder of the gunfire even in faraway London.

❛We saw the bombardment the Germans were getting. We thought it was a chance of getting our own back. Everyone was wildly 15 enthusiastic. Far less men went on sick parade. Nobody wanted to miss the fight.❜

Private Graham Williams, in a TV documentary.

On and on the guns went, day after day. The noise was terrible.

❛We couldn't speak, but it was an amazing 20 show. We stood behind the lines and watched the giant fireworks in the darkness. No one could live through that.❜

Lieutenant John Parker, in a TV documentary.

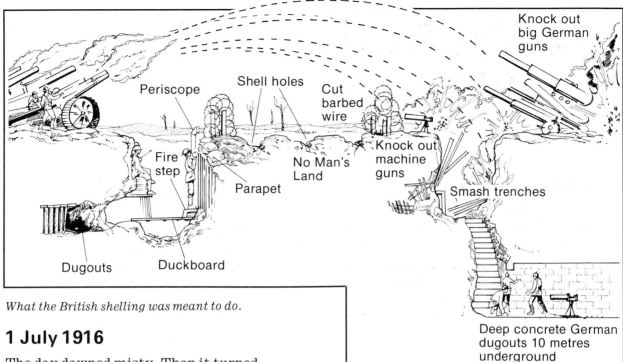

Knock out big German guns

Periscope

Shell holes

Cut barbed wire

Knock out machine guns

Smash trenches

Fire step

No Man's Land

Parapet

Dugouts

Duckboard

Deep concrete German dugouts 10 metres underground

What the British shelling was meant to do.

1 July 1916

The day dawned misty. Then it turned into a beautiful summer morning. The
25 British guns still thundered. The soldiers waited in the trenches.

‘ I thought of all the things I liked, and all the things I wanted to do. I told myself that it was all over but I was sick with sorrow. A rat ran
30 down the trench. The men stabbed at it, but it got away. In five minutes I would be dead. ’

John Masefield.

Then the guns stopped. The silence was strange. Soldiers' hearts were thumping.

‘ I kept reminding the men what to do, wiping
35 the mud off my rifle, over and over again. Five minutes to go . . . ’

R. H. Tawney (NCO). From Denis Winter,
'Death's Men: Soldiers of the Great War'
(Allen Lane, 1978).

The Hawthorn Redoubt – a German fort

Below ground the miners were busy. They had tunnelled towards the German trenches. They were going to blow the
40 Germans sky high.

‘ We were all miners. All mates at home. We played in the same football teams. We knew everyone. We worked in twos and threes. We laid the charges. You had to trust your mates. ’

Harry Hall, 1st Barnsley Pals, in a TV
documentary.

45 The mines blew.

‘ Like a gigantic sponge the earth rose into the air and with a grinding roar fell back again. ’

Geoffrey Malins, in a TV documentary.

The attack began at 7.30 am. Everyone heard the bang. The Germans knew what
50 it meant. The British were coming. The Germans raced from their deep, deep dugouts, far below ground. They raced up the steps. They raced into their trenches. They had not been blown to pieces. They
55 were ready.

‘ We pulled out the machine guns and rushed them up to the trenches. The British were coming – but slowly. They came on at a steady pace as if expecting to find nothing alive in our
60 front trenches. ’

'Going over the top.' The battle of the Somme, July 1916.

Then the Germans began firing. The British soldiers couldn't believe it. The Germans were not dead. On the British went.

65   ❛ In the flame and rolling smoke I see men arising and walking forward. Some men seem to pause with bowed heads. They sink to their knees, roll over and lie still. ❜

From Henry Williamson, 'Wet Flanders Plain' (Faber, 1929).

70   The German guns had not been knocked out. The deep German trenches had not been smashed. The barbed wire had not been cut by the British gunfire.

The end of the first day

On the first day of the battle of the Somme:

75   20,000 British soldiers were killed, and 37,000 British soldiers were wounded or taken prisoner.

2 July 1916

Horrified soldiers looked at the battlefield as the sun rose next day.

80   ❛ Hundreds of dead were strung out on the enemy wire like fish caught in a net. The Germans must have been reinforcing the wire for months. Daylight could barely be seen through it. How did the planners imagine that British soldiers would get through the German wire? Who told them that artillery gunfire would pound such wire to pieces? Any Tommy [British soldier] could have told them that shell-fire lifts wire up and drops it down, 90   often in a worse tangle than before. ❜

From George Coppard, 'With a Machine Gun to Cambrai' (HMSO, 1969).

The rest of 1916

General Haig was in charge of the British soldiers. He carried on just as before. Thousands and thousands of British soldiers pounded away at the Germans all 95   through the summer of 1916. The battle of the Somme ended in November 1916. Both sides were worn out.

General Ludendorff was in charge of the German army. He said: 'My army has 100   been fought to a standstill.' But so had the British army. The British soldiers had taken, at most, 15 kilometres of land from the Germans.

The British soldiers attack, 1 July 1916.

Wembley Stadium packed for a Bruce Springsteen concert on 4 July 1985. This gives *you an idea of the number of British casualties on the first day of the battle of the Somme.*

Many soldiers died on the barbed wire.

Things to Do

1 Fill in the gaps. (*Numbers in brackets refer to text line numbers.*)
   The ——————— (1) guns pounded the German ——————— (2). The big ————
   (2) blazed for ————— (2) days. The British guns stood almost side by side for
   —— (9) kilometres.

2 Write out the paragraph below. Choose the correct word from the brackets.
   The British soldiers watched the (biscuits/boxes/bombardment) the Germans were getting. The soldiers thought that (no one/everyone) could live through that.

3 How did John Masefield feel while he waited in the trenches (lines 27–31)?

4 How did R. H. Tawney show that he was nervous (lines 34–6)?

5 What happened to the British soldiers as they walked towards the German trenches (lines 61–8)?

6 Read the section headed '2 July 1916'. What does shell-fire do to wire?

7 How much land had the British taken from the Germans (line 102)?

15 Women at War

Many men became soldiers, sailors and airmen. They left their jobs. So women did men's jobs. They worked in factories. They made shells and bullets. They
5   worked on farms. They drove buses. They worked in steel mills. They also nursed.

Nursing

The Voluntary Aid Detachments were founded in 1910 by the Red Cross and St
10   John Ambulance Brigade. Each detachment had twenty-three members and a commander. Many, many women joined. They were known as VADs. They nursed in hospitals in Britain. They
15   nursed in hospitals in France and in other countries. They did other jobs too.

1917

The Women's Auxiliary Army Corps was started in February, 1917. The Women's Royal Naval Service was started in
20   November, 1917. Soon thousands of women joined the army and navy. They drove cars and lorries. They worked in army offices and canteens. This meant that more men could fight in the front
25   line.

The end of the war

It was 1918. By this time the Royal Air Force had started the Women's Royal Air Force section. There were 30,000 women in the WRAF.

Air damage on Etaples hospital. A number of Canadian nurses were killed in the raid.

American nurses arriving at a port in France in 1918.

Things to Do

1 Fill in the gaps. (*Numbers in brackets refer to text line numbers.*)
   So ————— (2) did men's jobs. They made —————— (4) and bullets. They worked on ————— (5). They worked in ————— (6) mills. They also ————— (7).

2 Look at the list of initials below. Some are real. Some are false. Write down the true initials that you have come across in this chapter and what they stand for.

WAAC	WREN	RWNA
GWV	VAD	WRAF
WAC	WCFM	VFT

◀ *Baroness T'Serclaes and Mairi Chisholm at their first-aid post in France in September 1917. They became well known for their work in the front line. It was unusual for women to be allowed that close to the fighting on the Western Front. One of them was badly gassed.*

VAD drivers repairing their ambulances and cars in France in 1918. Many ambulances were donated by groups of workers or by towns.

16 Horses in the War

The war was a war for animals, too. About 16 million animals were used in the war on all sides. These animals included dogs, pigeons, donkeys, mules, camels and
5 horses. Telephone lines were blown up. Wirelesses broke down. Signals could be seen by the enemy. So often soldiers, pigeons and dogs carried the messages.
 Mules and horses were used again and
10 again. They had many jobs.

Jobs for horses and mules

1 Large mules and small horses were used to pull field-guns and small carts carrying water, food, wood and other things.
15 2 Big horses were used to pull heavy guns and big carts.
 3 Small pack-horses and small mules carried bullets and shells in packs on their backs.
20 4 Riding horses were used for mounted soldiers

Remount department

The remount department was very big in the army. Each division (18,000 soldiers) needed 5,500 horses. Cavalry divisions
25 needed twice that number. Many soldiers worked in the department. Their job was to buy horses for the army. As the war went on they needed thousands and thousands of horses. They bought them
30 from all over the world. They bought mules in India and horses in South America. These animals were loaded into ships. Each ship carried between 600 and 800 horses. Sometimes a German
35 submarine sank a ship. All the horses were drowned.

This was a famous poster during the First World War. It was designed by an artist called Matania.

1 Why does he ask the reader to help the horse?
2 What does he ask the reader to join?
3 In what ways could raising money in the USA help horses in France? How would you set about organizing help for horses?
4 Look very carefully at the poster. Explain in class what has happened.
5 The blank space at the bottom of the poster is for the title. Write down your own title for it.
6 Do you think Matania loved horses? How do you know?

A horse and water cart sinking in mud, Ypres 1917. The horse has stepped off the fascine road (bundles of twigs laid to form a road). The rider is leaning down to release the horse. Usually the horse would be shot, but this one was lucky. Later photographs show that the soldiers pulled the horse out. The water cart sank.

Transport

Horses and mules pulled and carried and struggled through the dust of summer and the deep mud of winter. They carried
40 guns, shells, food and medicine from the trains to the soldiers in the front-line trenches. It was a dangerous job.

All the armies fighting used horses in this way. Horses pulled Red Cross carts
45 for the Russian army. They pulled guns for the German army. They carried French soldiers and British generals.

Care of horses

Horses had to be looked after night and day. They ate. They drank. They were
50 injured. They fell sick.

But the soldiers loved their horses. Often the soldier and his horse were together for days or weeks on end. They shared the wind and the rain. They were
55 hungry and cold together. They were both terrified in battle. They were bored when there was nothing to do. Looking after his horse gave the soldier a reason for living.

Veterinary care

60 Many horses were injured by guns. Many horses trod on loose nails and pieces of metal. Every week 400 horses had to be treated for cuts on their feet. Hungry horses sometimes ate the rugs off the
65 backs of their neighbours. They half choked. The veterinary surgeons looked after them.

The cavalry

Some soldiers fought on horseback. They were called cavalry. Most of the generals
70 in the First World War were cavalry men. Lieutenant Colonel E. G. French wrote in his memoirs in 1951:

⟨ Nothing in the wars of old or in those of modern times, has been found to equal the
75 devastating effect of lines of furiously charging horses. ⟩

Barbed wire, mud, machine guns and high explosives ripped these brave soldiers and horses to pieces.

Palestine

80 This was one place where the cavalry was successful. The British were fighting the Turks in Palestine. There were large areas of open sandy desert. It was 31 October 1917. Martin Balserini was an 85 Australian.

❝ We left in dark and we done 40 mile that night through desert. Then we camped in the day and then done another 40 mile without water and Beersheba was the only place with 90 water. If we couldn't have taken Beersheba those horses would have had to go another 30 mile and they wouldn't have done it.

Once we got going them horses galloped as fast as they could go and no one tried to keep 95 them back. When we got in there was no barbed wire just the Turks in the trenches. We were shooting from off the horses and the Turks were firing out of the trenches. We were on them and round them and shooting fit to 100 bust. It didn't last long. They chucked it in. ❞

The Royal Scots Greys. Horses will not drink polluted water. This could be very difficult when thousands of soldiers and animals were living close together.

1914–18

One million horses belonged to the British army between 1914 and 1918. Of those:

105 190,000 died of sickness, overwork and injury; and 60,000 were killed on the battlefield by bullet, shell or gas.

Things to Do

1 Fill in the gaps. (*Numbers in brackets refer to text line numbers.*)
About 16 –––––––– (2) animals were used in the war on all sides. These animals included dogs, pigeons, donkeys, –––––– (4), camels and –––––– (5).

2 Look at the section headed 'The cavalry'. Then write out the sentences below choosing the correct word from the brackets.
Some soldiers fought on horseback. They were called (caravans/cavalry/cats). Lieutenant Colonel E. G. French wrote in (1519/1915/1951).

A German transport horse. It was easy to gas your own soldiers and animals.

3 Do you think the cavalry could win a battle today? Talk about your answers in class.

4 Read what Martin Balserini said (lines 86–100).

   (a) How far did the soldiers and horses ride each night?

   (b) What did Beersheba have that the horses needed?

   (c) Why could the horses gallop right up to the Turks' trenches?

   (d) Was Balserini's cavalry charge successful?

This soldier and horse are so smart they must be on home service. On the man's arm is a wound stripe, long service stripes, marksman insignia and a lance corporal stripe. He has a wallet with personal belongings and a haversack on his back. He carries picketing pegs, brushes, gas mask, groundsheet (behind the saddle), white bag for food, food (a canvas bucket on the other side of the horse), flag, rifle in 'bucket' (other side), picketing rope, blanket under the saddle for the horse. A cavalry horse in the British army like this one carried about 140 kg in marching order.

5 Do the crossword. *(Numbers in brackets after clues refer to text line numbers. You will need to read the whole sentence to find the answer.)*

ACROSS

1 About 16 million animals were –––– in the war on all sides. (1)

3 Barbed wire, mud, machine guns and high explosives ripped these –––––– soldiers and horses to pieces. (77)

6 Riding –––––– were used for mounted soldiers. (20)

7 Horses pulled ––– Cross carts for the Russian army. (44)

8 Hungry horses sometimes ––– the rugs off the backs of their neighbours. (63)

10 ––– horses were used to pull heavy guns and big carts. (15)

11 Many horses were–––––––– by guns. (60)

13 The ––– was a war for animals, too. (1)

15 They fell––––. (50)

16 'Nothing in the wars of ––– or in those of modern times, has been found to equal the devastating effect of lines of furiously charging horses.' (73)

DOWN

2 We were –––––––– from off the horses and the Turks were firing out of the trenches. (96)

4 The –––––––––– surgeons looked after them. (66)

5 Horses and mules pulled and carried and struggled through the dust of summer and the –––– mud of winter. (37)

9 They pulled –––– for the German army. (45)

12 –––– ship carried between 600 and 800 horses. (33)

14 Every week 400 horses had –– be treated for cuts on their feet. (62)

17 Russia in 1917

By 1917 Russia had had enough. Nearly
two million soldiers had died. No one
knows how many ordinary people died of
hunger, cold and illness in Russia as the
5 armies retreated.

The people of Russia did not believe in
the tsar any more. They heard terrible
stories about the tsar's family. The tsar's
son had a blood disease. A strange monk
10 arrived at the palace. His name was
Rasputin. He made the tsar's son better.
The tsar's wife thought Rasputin was
wonderful. He was given great power.
Ordinary people in Russia thought this
15 was terrible. Rasputin could do anything.
No one could stop him. He gave important

Rasputin with admirers.

Russia in 1917.

jobs to weak men. Some men disagreed
with Rasputin. They lost their jobs. In
the end a group of important people got
20   together. They murdered Rasputin. They
said that they did it to save Russia.

March 1917

Nothing could save the tsar. He
abdicated. He stopped being the tsar.
Later the tsar and his family were shot.
25   A new government was set up. Soon it
was led by Kerensky.
Florence Farmborough went to listen
to Kerensky:

‘ At first glance he looked small and
30   insignificant. I remember clearly a feeling of
disappointment. Was this man really
Kerensky? He spoke for twenty minutes. He
came alive. The thousands of soldiers around
the hilltop listened in awe.
35   "You, free men of a free country; you will
fight for Russia, your Mother Country," he
urged.
"We are free men," the soldiers roared. "We
will fight! We will! We will!" ’

*From Florence Farmborough, ‘Nurse at the
Russian Front: A Diary of 1914–18’
(Constable, 1974).*

40   But the months passed. Still Russia did
badly in the war. Many soldiers lost
heart. Many listened to the Bolsheviks.

The Bolshevik revolution

Lenin led the Bolshevik party. He
promised:

45   ● to end the war;
● to give land to the people.

More and more soldiers listened. They
wanted peace now. They wanted land.
They wanted to go home. Thousands of
50   soldiers picked up their knapsacks. They
walked away from the trenches.
From November 1917 Lenin and the
Bolsheviks ruled Russia. Lenin ended the
war with Germany.

*Russian people living in the forest near Riga
during the war.*

*Lenin addressing a meeting in Petrograd (now
Leningrad) in November 1917.*

Deserting Russian soldiers have taken army food carts. Here they are being stopped by Russian and British officers who have arrived in armoured cars.

The treaty of Brest-Litovsk, March 1918

55 In March 1918 Russia and Germany signed an agreement to end the war. This was the treaty of Brest-Litovsk. In the treaty Russia agreed to give a great deal of land to Germany. Lenin did not care. He was
60 sure Russia would get the land back again.

Britain and France were horrified. They now faced Germany alone. Britain and France hoped that the USA would join
65 them in time.

Poster of a Russian worker, October 1917 (see question 3 in Things to Do).

18 War at Sea – Submarines

It was 1914. Submarines were fairly new in war. Germany built many submarines. A German submarine was called an *Unterseeboot* or U-boat. Germany wanted

5 to use its submarines to sink British ships.

Neutral ships

It was one thing for the Germans to sink British ships. After all Germany and Britain were at war. But Germany

10 wanted to stop all food and supplies reaching Britain. So Germany wanted to sink all ships sailing to Britain. The Germans wanted to sink Danish, Dutch and American ships. All these countries

15 were angry. The Americans were very angry. They had several rows with the Germans.

The *Lusitania*

One row was over the *Lusitania*. The *Lusitania* was a beautiful British

20 passenger ship. It sailed from New York in the USA on 1 May 1915. It was sailing to Britain. The day it sailed a German submarine had torpedoed an American ship. The Germans had also

25 warned that ships around Britain might be sunk.

No one took any notice. Who would sink

Ships came to Britain from all over the world. There were Dutch, Danish, French, American, Italian, Portuguese, South African and New Zealand ships. Look carefully at the map. You are a German U-boat commander. You want to sink ships coming to Britain. Where would you lie in wait to ambush these ships? Ships came through the Suez Canal and from the Mediterranean Sea too.

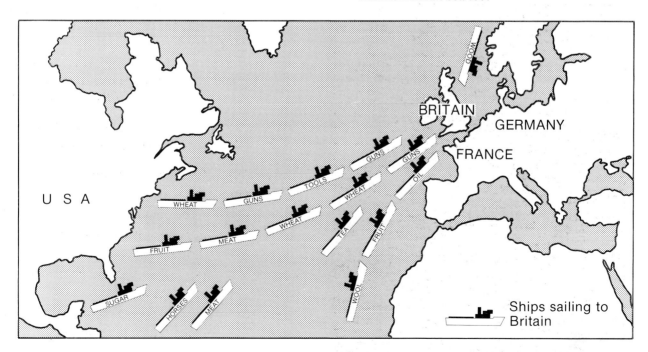

Ships sailing to Britain

a pleasure ship like the *Lusitania*? It had
nothing to do with the war. This was not

30 true. Deep in *Lusitania*'s hold were 4,200
cases of bullets. They were for British
guns. The *Lusitania* was carrying war
goods. Within a few days it was near
Britain. It was sailing close to Ireland.

On board U20 below the sea, 7 May

35 At 1.40 p.m. Captain Schweiger looked
through his periscope. He was delighted.
At last – here was the *Lusitania*. At
2.09 p.m. he took aim. He fired a torpedo.
At 2.10 p.m. the torpedo hit the *Lusitania*.

40 ‘ Hit starboard side, right behind the bridge.
An unusually strong explosion. ’

Ship's log (U20), 7 May 1915.

The torpedo had hit the bullets. In a few
minutes the ship leant over. People
screamed. They ran to the lifeboats.

45 Everything happened so fast. The ship
leant over more. Chairs, tables, plates
and suitcases shot down the slope.
'It's going to roll right over,' thought
Captain Schweiger. But it didn't.

50 Suddenly the big ship's bow went down. It
dived to the seabed. Its four great funnels
sank slowly from sight. It had taken 18
minutes to sink the *Lusitania*.
Lifeboats, bodies and swimmers

55 covered about a kilometre of sea. Rescue
boats steamed to help. But 1,198 people
drowned. Among them were 128
Americans. The USA was furious with
Germany. So was Britain.

The inquiry

60 There was a British inquiry into the
sinking. Several things were *not* said:

- No one said anything about the bullets
on board.
- No one said that the British navy

65 should have sent boats to protect the
Lusitania when it got near to Britain.
- No one asked why the *Lusitania* was not
sent to Britain by a less dangerous
route.

Germany and the USA

70 The USA was big and rich. Germany did
not want to fight the USA, too. So it used
submarines to sink only British ships.

1917

But by 1917 Germany was doing badly.
The war was still a stalemate. The

75 German army was not winning on land.
The German navy was bottled up. So the
Germans decided to attack all ships
coming to Britain. The Americans were
furious. This was the last straw. They

80 declared war on Germany.

April 1917

It was April 1917. The Germans sank 300
British ships in one month. Winston
Churchill said that there was only enough
food left in Britain to feed everyone for

85 six weeks. Something had to be done.

Peace?

Britain had fought for three years. People
were tired and sad. Soon they would be
starving. Perhaps Britain ought to make
peace with Germany. But the government

90 decided to carry on the war. The British
people did not want to give in. Soon the
American soldiers would arrive to help.
The British would hang on.

Look carefully at this British poster. ▶

1 *What is the name of the ship that is sinking?*
2 *Where did the* Lusitania *sail from on 1 May 1915 (read the section headed* Lusitania*)?*
3 *To which country was the* Lusitania *sailing?*
4 *Who sank the* Lusitania*?*
5 *Why was the USA furious?*
6 *Look at the drawing of the medal (in the corner of the poster). The Germans made the medal, so the British said. The medal celebrated the sinking of the* Lusitania*. The British secretly copied the medal. They sold many copies in Britain. 'Look,' said the British. 'How dreadful the Germans are. They are thrilled that they have drowned many people.' One side of the medal showed passengers buying their tickets for the journey on the* Lusitania*. Who is selling the tickets?*

The convoy system: beating the U-boats

Merchant ships sailed in groups.
95 Warships sailed with them. This was
called a convoy. The warships looked for
U-boats. Then they sank them. By 1918
few merchant ships were sunk by German
submarines. The convoy system worked.
100 The silent, deadly submarines were
defeated.

◄ *U-boats in Kiel Harbour, Germany.*

Things to Do

1 Fill in the gaps. (*Numbers in brackets refer to text line numbers.*)
Germany built many————— (2). A German submarine was called an *Unterseeboot* or U- ———— (4). It was one thing for the Germans to sink ——————
(8) ships. But Germany wanted to ————
(10) all food and supplies reaching
—————— (11). So Germany wanted to sink ——— (12) ships sailing to Britain.

2 Do the crossword. (*Numbers in brackets after clues refer to text line numbers. You will need to read the whole sentence to find the answer.*)

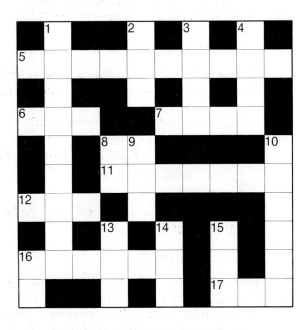

ACROSS
5 —————— were fairly new in war. (1)
6 Winston Churchill said that there was only enough food left in Britain to feed everyone for ——— weeks. (81)
7 Who would sink a pleasure ———— like the *Lusitania*? (27)
8 —— unusually strong explosion. (41)
11 He fired a ———————. (38)
12 ——— row was over the *Lusitania*. (18)
16 The Germans wanted to sink ——————, Dutch and American ships. (13)
17 It sailed from New York in the USA on 1 ——— 1915. (21)

DOWN
1 The —————— was a beautiful British passenger ship. (19)
2 The *Lusitania* was carrying ——— goods. (32)
3 The USA was big and ————. (70)
4 ———— in *Lusitania*'s hold were 4,200 cases of bullets. (30)
8 —— last – here was the *Lusitania*. (37)
9 But this was ——— true. (29)
10 The —————— system worked. (99)
13 At 2.10 p.m. the torpedo ——— the *Lusitania*. (39)
14 ——— silent, deadly submarines were defeated. (100)
15 He took ———. (37)
16 It had nothing to —— with the war. (28)

3 Look at the map on page 67. Then answer the following questions:
(a) What are the ships bringing to Britain?
(b) Why do you think the Germans wanted to sink ships going to Britain?

19 The USA and the First World War

August 1914

Woodrow Wilson was President of the
USA. He was very sad. Britain declared
war on Germany. Wilson loved Britain.
He admired Germany. But most of all he
5 wanted to keep the USA out of the war.
This was difficult.

Staying neutral

The USA was rich. It made many things.
For example, it made machines,
chemicals, guns, trains and ammunition.
10 The USA produced a great deal of food.
Britain and France needed to buy from
the USA. Germany needed to buy from
the USA. Wilson decided that the USA
must be neutral. It must sell things to
15 *both* sides. The USA must lend money to

The two-sided American approach to war.

both sides. That showed that the USA was
not taking sides. (Many Americans made
a lot of money, too!)

Britain's navy

Britain had many ships. Britain used its
20 ships against Germany. This meant that
Germany could not buy things from the
USA. Was this fair? Wilson decided he had
to leave Britain and Germany to fight it
out. The USA sold things to Britain
25 because British ships got to the USA.

The *Lusitania*

It was 1915. A German submarine sank the
Lusitania. The *Lusitania* was a big British
passenger ship. But there were 128
Americans on board. They were all
30 drowned. The American people were
upset. But they did not want to go to war.

1917

Two things happened in 1917 that made
the USA angry.

'Sink all ships'

First, Germany felt it was not winning
35 the war. Germany had to knock out
Britain and France. Germany decided to
attack *all* ships sailing to Britain. It used
submarines. The submarines sank
British, French, American, Dutch ships
40 and so on. America was furious.

The Zimmermann telegram

Zimmermann was the Foreign Secretary
of Germany. He sent a telegram to

Mexico. He wanted Mexico and Germany to be allies. He wanted Mexico to let
45 German submarines use Mexico as a base. Then after the war Germany would help Mexico take land from the USA.

Decoding

Zimmermann sent three telegrams. The telegrams were in code. But the British
50 were very good at working out German codes. They decoded all three telegrams. The British jumped for joy. They handed the telegrams to the Americans. The telegrams were published on 1 March.
55 Everyone read them in the newspapers.
      Theodore Roosevelt was an American politician. He said: 'If Wilson doesn't go to war now I shall skin him alive!'
      What could Wilson do? The American
60 people were horrified. They wanted to fight Germany.

6 April 1917

The USA declared war on Germany on 6 April 1917. Britain and France were

This poster reads 'U-boat attack!' Choose the correct word(s) from the brackets:

The poster is (British/American/German/ French). The captain is looking through a (power drill/stethoscope/periscope) he hopes to see a (ship/shop) carrying goods to (Bermuda/ Britain). He wants to (seek/sink) ships using (tree trunks/torpedoes/tarantulas).

delighted. Their armies were tired. They
65 had fought and died for three years. But now there was hope. The Americans were coming to help.
      Germany was afraid. Its army was tired, too. It did not have many soldiers
70 left. But Germany must attack France and Britain. Germany must win the war before the American soldiers arrived.

The doughboys

American soldiers were nicknamed 'doughboys'. They were healthy, fresh
75 and keen.
      Slowly the American doughboys began to arrive in France. The Americans had a small army. They had to recruit young men. They had to train them. They had to
80 gather the soldiers at the big American ports. Then the soldiers went on board ships. They sailed 4,800 kilometres to France.

The Germans attack, March–July 1918

The Germans attacked the French and
85 British. They drove them back. Perhaps the Germans could win the war before enough American soldiers arrived. But the British and French hung on. The Americans rushed more and more
90 soldiers to France. In July 1918 alone, 306,703 American soldiers landed in France.
      From July onwards, the British, French and Americans began to win.

Things to Do

1 Fill in the gaps. (*Numbers in brackets refer to text line numbers.*)
   Woodrow –––––– (1) was President of the ––– (2). Wilson loved –––––– (3). He admired –––––– (4). But most of all he wanted to keep the ––– (5) out of the war.

2 Discuss in class why the USA declared war on Germany. (Look for the two things that annoyed Americans – see lines 32–61).

3 Henry Lawson was a young lieutenant in the British army. He had retreated as the Germans attacked in March 1918. Now he was in the front line, holding it against the Germans.

‘ It was a warm June evening, and I was sitting quietly on the firestep reading. An American colonel came to visit our trench looking fresh and keen.

"Is this war, Mr Lawson?" he asked.

"Yes," I said.

"But it's very quiet. Where are the Germans?"

"About 70 yards [64 metres] over there," I pointed, keeping my arm low.

"But nothing's happening." I told him that neither us nor the Germans wasted ammunition.

"But this is war," he said.

I called for a spade. I dug out some earth and tossed it over the parapet. I knew a German sniper would see it. Then I held up the spade with its blade above the parapet. Within seconds there was a crack and a hole neatly drilled in the spade. The American looked at the spade and walked away without a word. ’

From Lieutenant Henry Lawson, 'Vignettes of the Western Front' (Positif Press, 1979).

(a) Who came to visit Lawson?

(b) Why do you think the American looked fresh and keen?

(c) How do you think Lawson would have looked to the American?

Woodrow Wilson leading a Liberty Loan parade (raising money for the war) in New York.

American soldiers arriving at Le Havre, France, on 12 July 1918. They were tall, healthy and keen. They were very different from the tired European soldiers who had been fighting for nearly four years.

(d) How far away were the Germans?

(e) Why did Lawson keep his arm low when he was pointing?

(f) Why did the American think that both sides should be shooting at each other?

(g) What reason did Lawson give for both sides not shooting all the time?

20 Tanks

Machine guns, barbed wire and big guns changed war. No soldiers could move forward. The guns were too powerful. The barbed wire was too thick. Winston

5   Churchill said: 'We went on fighting machine guns with the gallant chests of men.'

How could anyone win?

Several men thought of tanks. The

10   British built several tanks. Many generals thought the tanks were a waste of time. But some people in the government liked them. They said: 'You aren't winning the war. This new

15   machine might.'

This a Mark IV British tank. It was the most widely used tank in the First World War. It was nearly 8 metres long. It could cross a trench 3 metres wide.

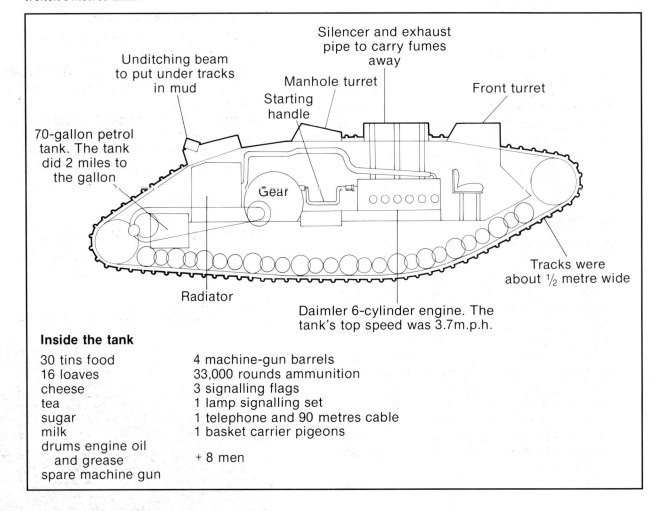

Unditching beam to put under tracks in mud

Silencer and exhaust pipe to carry fumes away

Manhole turret

Starting handle

Front turret

70-gallon petrol tank. The tank did 2 miles to the gallon

Gear

Tracks were about ½ metre wide

Radiator

Daimler 6-cylinder engine. The tank's top speed was 3.7 m.p.h.

Inside the tank

30 tins food	4 machine-gun barrels
16 loaves	33,000 rounds ammunition
cheese	3 signalling flags
tea	1 lamp signalling set
sugar	1 telephone and 90 metres cable
milk	1 basket carrier pigeons
drums engine oil and grease	
spare machine gun	+ 8 men

15 September 1916

A few tanks attacked the Germans on the Somme.

20 ❛There is not one of us who will ever forget his first ride in a tank. We couldn't stand up. The engine roared. We couldn't hear, nor could we see. It was almost completely dark inside. The tremendous jolt as we started and we were on our way. This was a great adventure.❜

Sergeant Littledale, Tank Corps. From Bryan Cooper, 'Ironclads of Cambrai' (Pan, 1970).

25 The tanks moved towards the German trenches. The German soldiers were terrified. They called the tanks 'devil's coaches'. The tanks broke through to the German trenches. But there were not 30 enough tanks. Many of the tanks broke down.

Passchendaele

Even worse was what happened at Passchendaele. Passchendaele was near Ypres. Britain had many new tanks. They 35 set off through the rain. They sank in the mud. Major Fuller was disgusted. Of course tanks could not work in a sea of mud. He said they must be used at Cambrai. They must have a fair trial.

Cambrai

40 Cambrai was chalkland. It was firm. No big guns had been used there. The land was smooth. But the Germans had built strong trenches. They were 6 metres wide. The barbed wire was 50 metres deep. It 45 was a forest of wire. But Fuller was sure his tanks could break through.

The trenches were too wide even for a tank to cross. But Fuller had an answer. The tanks carried huge bundles of 50 brushwood. They were called **fascines.** There were sixty or seventy bundles of wood in a fascine. The workshops worked day and night for three weeks. They made 350 fascines.

55 The tanks got ready. They waited in the woods. They waited for dawn. The big British guns started to shell the German guns. The tanks moved slowly forward.

The German trenches

Hans Hildemann was 19 years old. He was 60 in the front German trench. He was in a look-out post. 'You'll be all right,' his sergeant said. 'The British soldiers will never attack while their big guns are firing.' The sergeant went down to the 65 dugout. Hildemann was nervous. He heard a new noise. It was like an aeroplane. But there were no aeroplanes overhead. Then he saw it. It loomed out of the mist. It towered above him, blocking 70 out the sky. He couldn't move. Where had it come from? What was it? How had it got through the wire?

The tanks break through

The tanks rolled on. The soldiers came behind. They bombed the German 75 dugouts. They took prisoners. Sometimes a tank was hit and blew up. Sometimes a tank broke down.

By lunchtime the tanks had driven 10 kilometres into the German lines. The 80 Germans had run away. It was a huge victory. The news spread. The church bells were rung in London. Maybe the war would soon be over.

The German counterattack

The tanks had done their job. Many had 85 been destroyed. The others needed

Tank with fascine bundle.

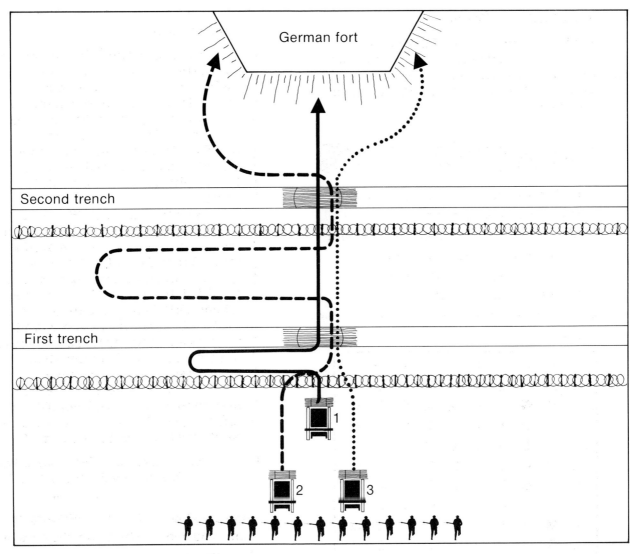

Major Fuller made a tank battle drill. He said tanks should work in threes:

Tank 1 *squashes wire, turns left and fires along first trench. Then carries on. Meanwhile*

Tank 2 *squashes wire, drops fascine in first trench, crosses first trench, turns left and fires along second trench. Then carries on.*

Tank 3 *squashes wire, crosses first trench, drops fascine in second trench, crosses trench.*

The three tanks join to attack the fort. Behind the tanks come soldiers.

servicing. They were loaded on to trains. Then the news came. The Germans were fighting back. The tanks were needed. The British soldiers fought hard. But the

90 Germans won back most of the land the tanks had gained.

But no one said tanks were useless any more. They were used again and again.

Amiens, 8 August 1918

First, the big British guns silenced the
95 German guns. This was the biggest tank attack yet. More than 600 British and French tanks attacked the Germans. The heavy Mark V tanks squashed flat the forests of barbed wire. The soldiers
100 walked behind. By night-time they had gone 10 kilometres. The Germans were on the run.

The end of the war

Tanks were important. They helped to
end the stalemate on the Western Front.
105 But no one had enough tanks. Perhaps
tanks would be used in large numbers in
the future.

Things to Do

1 Fill in the gaps. (*Numbers in brackets
   refer to text line numbers.*)
   Machine ———— (1), barbed ———— (1) and
   ——— (1) guns changed war. No
   ———————— (2) could move forward.
   Several men thought of ————— (9).
2 Look at the word square. Copy it into your
   book.

T	F	U	L	L	E	R	X	M	M
C	A	M	B	R	A	I	A	I	A
H	S	N	L	B	M	A	S	E	C
U	C	Q	K	V	I	T	D	Z	H
R	I	L	N	S	E	R	K	J	I
C	N	U	O	Y	N	R	A	I	N
H	E	G	U	N	S	O	M	M	E
I	C	E	M	U	D	W	I	R	E
L	M	A	R	K	V	O	P	G	Q
L	S	C	H	A	L	K	N	E	S

Find the following words in the square.
Cross out the words as you find them. The
words can run in any direction.

Fuller	Somme	fascine	tanks
Churchill	chalk	London	wire
hear	Cambrai	machine	Amiens
rain	Mark V	gun	mud

3 The following letter about the battle of
   Arras in 1917 is from Captain N. F.
   Humphreys to a friend, Colonel Clarke.
   Captain Humphreys was killed at the
   battle of Amiens in 1918.

'Dear Clarke,

We had a jolly time. But what a trip
to the starting line! Listen. First
night: broken fan-drive chain.
Mended it with a nail from a ration
box! Second night: broken main drive
flexible coupling. Fitted the spare
one. Third night: Diff. lock jammed
in. Sat tight and waited for dawn.
Mended diff. lock. Off we went. Late of
course.

But all ready to start. We had a
jolly run to our front line. Everyone
inside merry and bright. Then off we
went. Bundled over two German
trenches and hit a topping target in
the third. It was a machine-gun post.
Whoomph! Then over a hill and into
a ditch! Other tanks passed us and
soldiers walking and there we were on
our side. I squeezed out and took a
stroll to see how our chaps were
doing. But a sniper did the dirty on
me and I was back in my comfy
armour-plated bus in no time. There
we stayed till we got pulled out!'

*From Peter Liddle, 'Testimony of War,
1914–18' (Michael Russell, 1979).*

Read the sentences below, choosing the
words you think are best from the ones in
the brackets.

We had a (difficult/easy) time getting to
the starting line. We kept (rushing ahead/
breaking down). We were (late/early), of
course. We had a (miserable/fast/jolly)
run to our front line. We got over (one/
two/three] German trenches. We hit a
(machine-gun post/fort/brick wall). Then
we fell into a (ditch/pond/river). I got out
but a (piper/sniper/wiper) shot at me.
Quickly I got back into my (trench/lorry/
tank) and we stayed put till we got
(pulled out/blown up).

21 1917 and 1918

The war dragged on. It was April 1917. The
British attacked the Germans at Arras.
The French attacked the Germans, too.
But it was a disaster. Again thousands of
5 French soldiers died.

Mutiny

The French soldiers had had enough.
Parts of the French army mutinied. They
threw down their guns. They refused to
fight. For miles the French trenches were
10 empty. Luckily the Germans did not
know. Quickly General Pétain was put in
charge of the French army. At least the
soldiers trusted him.
    Fifty-five French soldiers were
15 executed. At the same time Pétain said
soldiers must have more leave, better
food and more rest. The mutiny was over.

Passchendaele, July 1917

The British said they would attack the
Germans again. This would keep the
20 Germans busy. It would help the French.
    The attack was terrible. It was at
Passchendaele, near Ypres. The generals
who planned the attack were a long way
behind the front lines. They ordered the
25 big guns to fire on the German trenches.
The weather was very wet. The British
soldiers were told to advance.

    ‘The rain was as heavy as ever when we
    moved off along the duckboard track. For
30   miles around us there was an endless chain of
    shell holes, filled with slimy water. The shells
    had ploughed up every yard of earth. Only
    sludge, stumps of trees and bits of bodies
    stuck out of the sea of mud.’

*From Lieutenant Henry Lawson, ‘Vignettes of
the Western Front, 1917–18’ (Positif Press,
1979).*

35   The battle of Passchendaele went on.
The British lost 300,000 soldiers. The
Germans lost 200,000 soldiers. The
battlefield became a stinking grave.

*Passchendaele. Soldiers walking on
duckboards.*

40 By November it was nearly over. An important officer came to look at the battlefield. He had helped the generals to plan the battle. He stood on a small hill and burst into tears: 'Did we send men to fight in this?' he asked.

The battle of Cambrai

45 ❛Zero was at 6.30 a.m. on 20 November. I shall never forget. We heard the sound of tank engines warming up. The first light of dawn was showing. We stood waiting for the big bang at the end of the countdown. Lieutenant
50 Garbutt and Seargeant Critcher were standing near me. At last the lieutenant began to count. He was bang on. In a flash the black sky behind us was ablaze. Terrible thunder swept along the 8-mile [about 13 kilometres] front.
55 Shells screamed over. The need for keeping quiet was over. We exploded in a babble of excitement. Surely we had more guns going than ever before.

We saw the tanks coming, looking like giant
60 toads at the top of the slope. The big guns stopped firing. Down swept the tanks.

This was the order scribbled out by General Elles the night before Cambrai. He did lead his tanks into battle. He stood in the manhole on

At zero plus one we moved forward. Rushed forward behind the tanks. The tanks had taken all fighting for an hour. We ran across no
65 man's land. The German wire had been dragged about like old curtains. There wasn't a German in sight.❜

From George Coppard, 'With a Machine Gun to Cambrai' (HMSO, 1969).

What a joy! Winning a battle at last. In London the church bells rang out. It was
70 to celebrate winning the battle of Cambrai. But the joy did not last long. The Germans struck back. They retook all the land that the tanks had won.

1918

Something was different about 1918. The
75 Americans had joined the war. They were on the British and French side. Soon American soldiers would arrive in France.

Russia had left the war. It had been
80 defeated by Germany. So Germany took soldiers away from the Eastern Front. It sent them to fight on the Western Front.

top of the tank carring the red, green and brown flag of the new Tank Corps.

Special Order No. 6

1 Tomorrow the Tank Corps will have the chance for which it has been waiting for many months, to operate on good going in the van of battle.
2 All that hard work and ingenuity can achieve has been done in the way of preparation.
3 It remains for unit commanders and for tank crews to complete the work by judgement and pluck in the battle itself.
4 In the light of past experience I leave the good name of the Corps with great confidence in their hands.
5 I propose leading the attack of the centre division.

Hugh Elles
Commanding Tank Corps

19 November 1917

Distribution to Tank Commanders.

The Germans attack, March 1918

The Germans wanted to win the war
quickly. They were short of food. The
85   Americans were coming. The Germans
had to defeat Britain and France before
thousands of American soldiers arrived.
The Germans pushed back the British. It
was May. The Germans pushed back the
90   French. General Foch was in charge of
the French and British armies.

July 1918

The German army could not be stopped.
It was closer to Paris than ever before.
But the Germans had gone too far. They
95   had no more soldiers. The American
soldiers had reached France. About
50,000 American soldiers arrived each
week.
        It was 18 July. The French, British and
100   Americans fought back. The Germans
retreated.

Revolution in Germany

The German people were starving.
German sailors refused to fight any more.
Germany decided to give in. It sent two
105   men to offer the French, British and
Americans an armistice or truce. They
signed an armistice in General Foch's
railway carriage. Germany had to give up
everything. It had lost the war.
110   The German kaiser had run away from
Germany a few days before the armistice.
He went to the Netherlands.

Things to Do

1   Fill in the gaps. (*Numbers in brackets
    refer to text line numbers.*)
    It was April ———— (1). The British
    attacked the Germans at ————— (2). But
    it was a ———————— (4). Thousands of
    British and French soldiers died. The

————— (6) soldiers had had enough.
Parts of the French army ———————— (7).
The British attacked the Germans again.
They attacked at ————————————— (22).

2   How many French soldiers were executed
    after the mutiny?
3   What did Pétain say the French soldiers
    must have?
4   What was the weather like at
    Passchendaele?
5. What was different about 1918?
6. Why did the Germans want to win the
    war quickly?
7   Look at 'Special Order No. 6' on page 79.
    Then answer the questions:
    (a)   What is the date of the order?
    (b)   Who is the order to be sent to?
    (c)   Read point no. 1. What two things
          does Elles say the Tank Corps has
          been waiting for?
    (d)   Look at point no. 2. Give one
          example of the 'ingenuity' of the Tank
          Corps in solving a problem (see
          Chapter 18 on tanks).
    (e)   Look at point no. 3. What do unit
          commanders and tank crews need in
          battle?
    (f)   Does Elles have confidence in his
          tank corps?
    (g)   Imagine you are a tank commander.
          Would you:
          (i)   read the order out to your soldiers
                that night? or
          (ii) put it carefully in your pocket as
                a souvenir?
          Give a reason for your answer.
    (h)   Why do you think many unit
          commanders did not agree with point
          no. 5?

22 War in Other Parts of the World

Turkey

Turkey was afraid of Russia. It thought Russia wanted more land around the Black Sea. So Turkey joined the war on the side of Germany. Turkey closed the
5 Dardanelles. This meant that British and French ships could not reach Russia. They could not send guns and ammunition to Russia. The British and French tried to force Turkey to re-open
10 the Dardanelles. They failed. (See chapter 11.)

Turkey and Russia

The Turks attacked the Russians. They were defeated. About 30,000 Turks froze to death in the Caucasus mountains in
15 Russia. The Russian soldiers counted the bodies.

The Suez Canal

Britain controlled the Suez Canal. Hundreds of British ships used the canal. It was a short cut to India and the Far
20 East. From 1914 to 1916 there were many British soldiers guarding it. Britain was afraid Turkey might attack the canal.

Oil

Britain was also interested in oil. There were oilfields in Persia (now called Iran).
25 Britain sent soldiers to hold the oilfields. They stopped the Turks getting the oil. The soldiers also stopped the Turks reaching the Indian Ocean.

The Arabs

Many Arabs lived in the Turkish empire.
30 They wanted to be free. Britain decided to help the Arabs.

The deal

The Arabs promised to attack Turkey. The British promised to help the Arabs make new, free Arab countries after the
35 war.

Lawrence of Arabia

T. E. Lawrence was British. He led the Arabs. He was clever. He knew that Arabs were not good soldiers. They were not well disciplined. But they were brave.
40 They were fierce. They were good guerrilla soldiers.

Lawrence of Arabia.

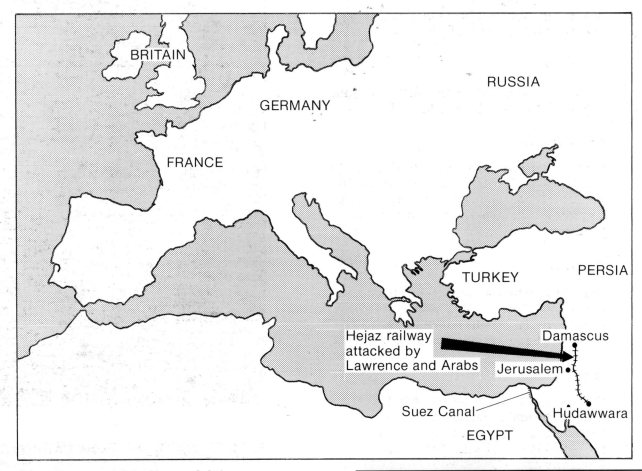

Where Lawrence of Arabia was fighting.

Lawrence also knew something else. He
knew how important the Hejaz railway
was to the Turks. The railway carried
45   Turkish goods, guns and soldiers.
Lawrence led the Arabs in attack after
attack on the Hejaz railway. They rode
camels. They crossed kilometres of hot,
dusty desert. They put dynamite under
50   the railway lines. They blew up the
Turkish trains.

General Allenby

General Allenby led the British army in
Palestine. He supported Lawrence and
the Arabs. Meanwhile he attacked the
55   Turks with British soldiers. They took
Jerusalem in 1917. Allenby finally
defeated the Turks in October 1918. All
the time Lawrence and his guerilla Arabs

*General Allenby in Jerusalem on 11 December
1917. He is listening to the reading of the
Proclamation of Occupation in seven
languages.*

Italian soldiers carrying packs and guns on ▶ their backs during fighting in the Alps.

60 helped. They stopped Turkish goods, guns and soldiers travelling on the railway.

After the war

Sadly, the British did not keep their promise. The British and French wanted the Arab lands themselves. They did not help the Arabs to make new, free Arab
65 countries.

Africa

Germany owned some land in Africa. Britain and France attacked German land in Africa. At the end of the war Germany had to give up all land in Africa.

Italy

70 Italy was not sure whether to join the war. In the end it decided to join with France, Britain and Russia. Italy reckoned it would win. It thought Germany and Austria would lose the war.
75 Then Italy could get land from Austria.

Caporetto

The Italian armies had a bad time. They fought in the mountains. They fought along the river Isonzo. The Austrians were on the other side of the river. The
80 months went by. Someone said: 'To defeat the Austrians we must get across the river. To get across the river we must first defeat the Austrians.'
    It was 1917. The Italians fought the
85 Austrians and Germans at Caporetto. The Italians collapsed.

Vittorio Veneto

Britain and France sent soldiers to help Italy. Finally the Italians won. This was at the battle of Vittorio Veneto. It was
90 1918.

Things to Do

1 Fill in the gaps. (*Numbers in brackets refer to text line numbers.*)
   Turkey was afraid of ────── (1). It thought Russia wanted more land around the ───── (3) Sea. So Turkey joined the war on the side of ─────── (4).
       Italy was not sure whether to join the ─── (71). In the end it decided to join with France, Britain and ────── (72). Italy reckoned it would win. It thought Germany and Austria would ──── the war (74). Then ───── (75) could get land from Austria.

2. Read the section headed 'The deal'. What did the Arabs promise to do? What did the British promise to do?

23 The End of the War

The collapse of Germany and its allies, 1918

See map below and answer the questions.

Look carefully at the map. Then answer the following questions:

1. *Which countries make up the central powers?*
2. *Which countries make up the allies?*
3. *Talk in class about why it became obvious that Germany could not go on fighting after 11 November 1918.*

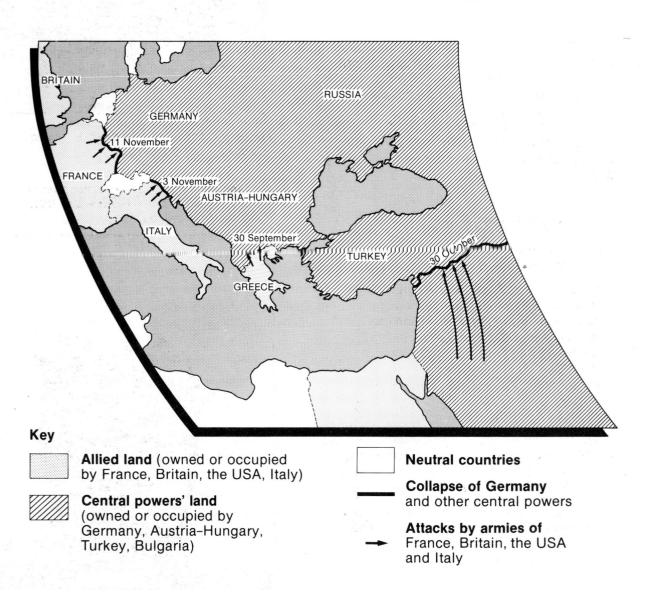

Key

Allied land (owned or occupied by France, Britain, the USA, Italy)

Central powers' land (owned or occupied by Germany, Austria-Hungary, Turkey, Bulgaria)

Neutral countries

Collapse of Germany and other central powers

Attacks by armies of France, Britain, the USA and Italy

The Armistice, 11 November 1918

It was eleven o'clock in the morning. It was the eleventh day. It was the eleventh month. The guns stopped firing. The war was over.

The German kaiser

The kaiser packed his bags. He left Germany before the Armistice. He went to live quietly in the Netherlands. He liked gardening.

The peace

But what about peace? What was going to happen now? Europe had been torn to shreds. Nothing could ever be the same again. The leaders of the great countries had to try to make a new Europe.

First, they had to make sure Germany was crushed. It must not rise again to fight.

Terms of the Armistice

These are some of the things that Germany had to agree to:

1 to take German soldiers out of Belgium, France and Luxemburg.
2 to give back to France the area of Alsace–Lorraine. (This was land Germany had taken from France in 1870.)
3 to surrender in good working order:

5,000 guns	5,000 lorries
25,000 machine guns	all submarines
3,000 trench mortars	6 battle cruisers
1,700 aeroplanes	10 battle ships
5,000 steam locomotives	8 light cruisers
150,000 wagons	50 destroyers

4 allow allied soldiers to occupy land in Germany. They occupied the left bank of the river Rhine.
5 to pay for damage done in the war.

The Germans agreed to surrender in November 1918 in a railway carriage.

The shooting stopped at the eleventh hour of the eleventh day of the eleventh month 1918. Many people celebrated with great joy.

War damage

This was a terrible problem. Germany had occupied part of France for four years.

War deaths

40   Millions of soldiers died. No one could bring them back. Millions of people lost their homes. Millions of soldiers were disabled. Millions of families had lost fathers, sons, brothers, boyfriends and

War damage to Britain was not so great. Some bombing and loss of ships and trade hurt Britain. The cost of the war hurt Britain too.

45   husbands. It was a terrible war.

What the leaders wanted

Clemenceau was Prime Minister of France. France had suffered dreadfully. Clemenceau wanted two things. First, he wanted to make Germany weak.
50   Secondly, he wanted to have revenge on Germany.

   Lloyd George was Prime Minister of Britain. He wanted to keep Germany weak. But he wanted to be fair. He said
55   that it was no use to want revenge. That

It had borrowed money from the USA. Britain was still paying back this money in the 1950s.

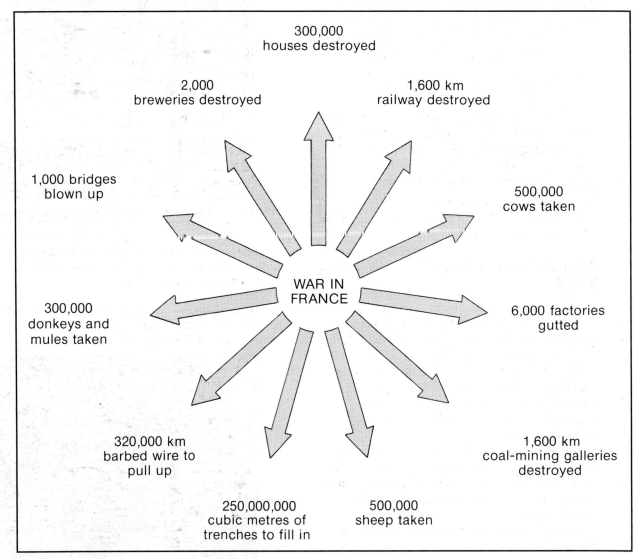

300,000 houses destroyed

2,000 breweries destroyed

1,600 km railway destroyed

1,000 bridges blown up

500,000 cows taken

WAR IN FRANCE

300,000 donkeys and mules taken

6,000 factories gutted

320,000 km barbed wire to pull up

1,600 km coal-mining galleries destroyed

250,000,000 cubic metres of trenches to fill in

500,000 sheep taken

was childish. Germany was a great country. If it was utterly crushed, the German people would hate Britain, France and the USA. The Germans would hate all of Europe. They would work and struggle to be great again. They might go to war again. The peace treaty must be firm but not too tough.

Wilson was President of the USA. He wanted to end war forever. He wanted everyone to be free. He had some ideas. He made a list of his ideas. It was called the **Fourteen Points.**

The Fourteen Points

These are some of the Fourteen Points:

1 Wilson wanted all countries to talk openly. He thought *secret* talks led to *secret* treaties. Then two or three countries ganged up together. They often went to war with another country.

2 He wanted all countries to trade freely.

3 He wanted all countries to be free. He wanted them to rule themselves (look at the map on page 88).

4 He wanted all countries to disarm.

Wilson's ideas were good. But they did not work well. Why do you think his ideas did not work well?

The peace conference, 28 June 1919

All the leaders argued about what should be done to Germany. Then they met at Versailles in France. The Germans had to sign the peace treaty. It was tough.

Two things stood out. First, Germany had to pay for war damage. This was damage to all the winning countries. Secondly, Germany had to say it had caused the war.

Apart from this, Germany lost all its land in other countries. It lost an eighth of its own land. It was not allowed to have a navy. It was allowed to have only a small army.

Lloyd George was unhappy. This was not a fair peace.

LANDES-KRIEGSFÜRSORGE-AUSSTELLUNG POZSONY JULI-AUGUST 1917

A poster advertising a National Exhibition for War Relief held in Pozsony and Bratislava, a part of the old Austro–Hungarian empire that became Czechoslovakia.

War memorials were built in many towns and villages. They reflect the shock, sorrow and horror of ordinary people about the war.

President Wilson encouraged freedom. Many
small countries were made. They were free to
rule themselves. For example, the Austrian
empire was broken up. Four small countries
were formed. These were Hungary, Austria,
Czechoslovakia and Yugoslavia.

The League of Nations

100 The League of Nations was set up. Its job
was to see that the Treaty of Versailles
was kept. It also was supposed to stop
war. If countries argued with each other
they went to the League of Nations in
105 Switzerland. The League decided what
should be done. It never worked well. For
one thing the USA was fed up with
Europe. It refused to join the League of
Nations.

PEACE AND FUTURE CANNON FODDER

The Tiger: "Curious! I seem to hear a child weeping!"

*This cartoon shows the French leader,
Clemenceau (nicknamed the Tiger) in the
front. In the background is Lloyd George. The
man in glasses is Woodrow Wilson. The
cartoon was drawn by an artist called Will
Dyson. What is he saying about the Treaty of
Versailles? Was he right or wrong?*

Things to Do

1 Fill in the gaps. (*Numbers in brackets
refer to text line numbers.*)
Europe had been torn to shreds. The
——————— (12) of the great countries had
to try to make a new —————— (13). First,
they had to make sure ——————— (14) was
crushed. It must not rise again to —————
(16).
2 Who was Clemenceau?
3 What two things did Clemenceau want?
4 Who was Lloyd George?
5 What two things did Lloyd George want?
6 What did Lloyd George say about
revenge?
7 Talk in class about what Lloyd George
said would happen if Germany was
utterly crushed. Could you have made a
better peace settlement?
8 Discuss in class why you think
Clemenceau may have wanted more
revenge on Germany than Lloyd George
and Wilson.

Index